Department of the Environment

Patterns and Processes of Urban Change in the United Kingdom

Reviews of Urban Research

Tony Fielding
Susan Halford

Centre for Urban and Regional Research
University of Sussex

ACTION FOR CITIES

LONDON: HMSO

© Crown copyright 1990
First published 1990

ISBN 0 11 752298 8

Other titles in the *Reviews of Urban Research Series:*

U.S. Experience in Evaluating Urban Regeneration   *ISBN 0 11 752280 5*   (1990) £7.70
Urban Labour Markets (forthcoming)

Note: A full list of titles in the Inner Cities Research Programme series is available from:

Inner Cities Directorate
Room P2/101B
Department of the Environment
2 Marsham Street
London SW1P 3EB

PREFACE

This report, commissioned by the Department of the Environment's Inner Cities Directorate, is the product of collaborative research. It was managed by Tony Fielding, Lecturer in Geography, and Susan Halford, Research Fellow, of the Centre for Urban and Regional Research at the University of Sussex.

Other members of the Centre also contributed to the writing of the report. They included: Peter Ambrose, Lecturer in Urban Studies; Mike Barrow, Lecturer in Economics; Peter Dickens, Lecturer in Urban Studies; Simon Duncan, Research Fellow (Lecturer in Geography, LSE); Mick Dunford, Lecturer in Geography; Peter Saunders, Professor of Sociology (Director of CURR); Mike Savage, Research Fellow (Lecturer in Sociology, Keele); and Andrew Sayer, Lecturer in Geography.

The review relied heavily on the co-operation of many people who generously gave of their time to be interviewed and to provide information. We would like to express our appreciation to all those who helped in this way, and to the Department's Nominated Officers, Stephen Batey and Graham Haughton, for their advice and support.

CONTENTS

EXECUTIVE SUMMARY

ES1 This report reviews the very extensive literature, published mostly during the last ten years, on urban change in the UK since 1971. Sixty studies have been selected from a bibliography of over 3000 items to illustrate the range of topics and perspectives represented in the literature. Summaries of the main findings of these studies are integrated into the text.

ES2 The structure of the report is explained in Figure 1 below. Urban change is regarded as being composed of three elements:

(i) changes in land use and built form, and in the spatial structure of the urban system;

(ii) changes in the nature and patterns of work and employment; and

(iii) changes in politics, culture and household and community relations.

Research on these aspects of urban change is reviewed in Chapters 1, 4, and 7 respectively. However, much recent research makes claims about the influence of one of these dimensions of urban change on one of the others — hence the six remaining Chapters.

Chapter 1

ES3 This Chapter focuses on research into the growth and decline of towns and cities in the UK (as measured by their population sizes), and on changes in urban land use and built form. There is a wealth of research on patterns of urban, rural and regional population change. Much of it shows that counterurbanization has characterised population redistribution in the UK since 1970. Large cities have tended to lose population through net migration losses while free-standing provincial cities, small and medium-sized towns and many rural areas have gained. It also shows that there was a bias towards growth in the southern part of the UK, and for growth to be concentrated in suburban and peri-urban areas while decline was concentrated in the inner city.

ES4 Recent studies of internal migration based upon the National Health Service Central Register data show that the rates of counterurbanization, suburbanization and inner city decline tended to be lower in the 1980s than in the 1970s. They also show that while the industrial heartland lost throughout the period 1975–86, peripheral areas changed from net gainers to net losers, and London changed from being a major net loser to being almost in balance in the early-mid 1980s.

ES5 This picture is backed up by research on 'rating places' which uses a wide range of variables including population change. This research confirms that the 1980s have seen a concentration of prosperity and growth in the south, and of poverty and decline in the north. It identifies an area of growth around and to the west of London, and shows that although there are certain areas in the north which are prosperous and growing, all the main cities of northern and western Britain perform less well than the median for Britain as a whole. Above all, it shows that there is a positive association between prosperity and growth, which means that a spatial polarisation in living standards is taking place.

ES6 Despite these geographical shifts in population, the evidence seems to suggest that at a broad regional scale, land use patterns have been relatively stable in the post-war period (due in part to support for agriculture and planning restraint in rural areas). This is so despite significant rates of suburbanization in the 1950s, 60s and early 70s, and the building of new towns and motorways. In contrast, at the urban scale, recession and technological changes (such as those affecting large ports) have resulted in major changes in land use and built form, notably an increase in derelict land in inner city areas. Recent research has shown how the special characteristics of the inner city land market produce high land prices which then deter the redevelopment of these derelict sites.

ES7 Research also asserts that land use patterns in the city reflect the relationships which pertained at the time of the areas' original development. These relationships get 'frozen' into the present-day spatial structure of the city in the form of street layouts, building densities, plot sizes etc., and in this way can affect the pace and nature of present-day urban change.

ES8 Our evaluation of the research reviewed in this Chapter is:

(i) that the literature on population redistribution is long on description but short on explanation;

(ii) that the urban life cycle model which purports to explain the patterns and processes of decentralisation and reconcentration does nothing of the sort; it is analytically unhelpful except in so far as it emphasises the importance of relative location;

(iii) that little good quality research has been carried out on changes in land use and built form, perhaps because of the paucity of reliable data on this subject.

Chapter 2

ES9 This Chapter examines research which claims that it is the physical structure of the urban system, or of a city, or of an area within the city which explains the patterns of job opportunities and employment change. Four claims of this nature were selected for special attention. In the first it was argued that unemployment in Britain was unnecessarily high due to the low mobility of labour which in turn was a result of the way in which the housing and social security systems allowed people to remain in the northern and western regions when the jobs for them were located in the south. The strength of this argument lies in the evidence on the association between geographical mobility and housing tenure, which shows that local authority tenants are particularly immobile.

ES10 This line of argument, however, is highly controversial, as is the second claim that cities are 'unfairly structured' and that this operates to disadvantage women in the labour market. According to this view, suburban location, especially in planned new towns, places women in a poor position to gain access to jobs, and especially to jobs which match their abilities and qualifications, yet permits them to maintain their 'dual role' as employees and as the main source of domestic labour in the household.

ES11 Just how difficult it is to determine the effects of physical structures and relative location on economic performance is demonstrated by the problems of estimating the size and distribution of the costs and benefits deriving from a major infrastructure investment such as the building of the Channel Tunnel.

ES12 Despite this many researchers subscribe to the theory that it is site constraint problems in the largest UK cities which largely explains the urban to rural shift in manufacturing employment so evident in the 1960s and 70s. This is contested by those who argue for the importance of labour force characteristics in affecting the rate and direction of industrial decentralisation, and by those who place redistribution trends within the context of corporate restructuring in the face of heightened international competition.

ES13 Our evaluation of the research reviewed in this Chapter is:

(i) that spatial structures and built forms do indeed become increasingly disfunctional with the passage of time, and that patterns of urban change today will partly reflect the attempts by economic actors to avoid the disadvantages of working within these outmoded structures;

(ii) but that there has been a tendency to place too much weight on this line of argument, to the exclusion of almost all other considerations. This criticism applies in particular to the attempts to explain unemployment in terms of low spatial mobility associated with a maldistributed housing stock, and the deindustrialisation of the major cities in terms of inner city built form obsolescence.

Chapter 3

ES14 This examines literature on the role of housing and built form in shaping social relationships. The debate about the role of spatial structures in determining social relations, sometimes couched in the language of 'environmental' or 'architectural determinism', has a long history. Recently this debate was re-opened in a highly charged way by the assertion that urban social problems in the inner areas of British cities are a result of the physical environments created by the 'modern movement' in architecture and planning. More specifically, indicators of social malaise such as vandalism and children taken into care were found to correlate with design factors such as numbers of dwellings in a block, height of the blocks, the extent to which they were linked to each other and so on. The interpretation placed upon this finding is that it is possible to solve or alleviate problems such as high crime rates by redesigning inner city environments.

ES15 Research on housing and race, although drawing upon very different concepts and theories, also emphasises the significance of the built environment in affecting life chances. It shows that despite legislation against racial discrimination and the fact that the majority of black people are now long standing residents of the UK, racial disadvantage in housing persists. Black people live in older and less desirable housing in both the public and the private sectors of the housing market, as tenants they pay higher rent, and as potential purchasers of housing they face more difficulty in obtaining mortgage finance, and tend to finish up owning property in inner urban areas which is costly to maintain and slow to increase in value. A major theme of recent writing has been that, as with gender inequality, racial inequality is not just reflected in the housing situations that black people find themselves in, it is also actively sustained and reproduced by the housing system.

ES16 But perhaps the area of debate about the role of housing and built form in shaping social relations which has attracted the most academic attention is that which focuses on the social significance of owner-occupation. Although it is conceded that home ownership is not a homogeneous category, many researchers now claim that it does (did?) produce substantial economic advantages, and does allow many people to give expression to deeply held values of independence and autonomy. To this extent tenure differences are said to generate new lines of inequality and cleavage in our society, and the division between a relatively privileged stratum of home owners and the increasingly marginalised stratum of poor council tenants is thought to be widening. Council tenancy is seen to be increasingly associated with indicators of deprivation such as poverty, unemployment, broken families, ethnic minorities and the elderly.

ES17 Our evaluation of the literature reviewed in this Chapter is:

(i) that a strong case had been made to support the contention that owner-occupation does confer social advantage on many people, and does allow the expression of individual identity and independence (though usually at the price of debt encumbrance); and

(ii) that although the architectural determinism contained in recent research on crime and vandalism in high rise estates is quite unacceptable, there is much yet to be learnt about the ways in which we are socially and psychologically affected by the material contexts of our lives.

Chapter 4

ES18 This Chapter reviews research on patterns and processes of urban employment change in the UK. This is, by a significant margin, the most intensively studied aspect of urban change in the recent period. As a result it is not easy to express the results of this research in a small number of sentences. The main empirical findings were as follows:

(i) a rapid decline in manufacturing employment from the late 1960s until the late 1980s at the national level, made up of massive declines in the major cities (including London), slower declines in many medium-sized towns and some growth in many small towns and rural areas;

(ii) differential job loss between industrial sectors, but declines by no means confined to the heavy industries such as coal mining, steel manufacture and shipbuilding, nor to the traditional 'problem' regions dominated by these industries; thus many of the cities associated with the consumer goods boom of the 1950s and 1960s such as London, Birmingham and Coventry, also experienced rapid job losses in manufacturing industry;

(iii) a growth in female employment, much of it part-time; this was partly associated with branch plant investment in the 1960s and early 1970s in industrial regions such as South Wales and the North East, and in small and medium sized towns in rural areas, but it was mostly and more generally associated with an increase in service employment;

(iv) service sector employment growth was not enough at the national level to offset the massive declines during the 1970s and early 1980s in manufacturing industry, but it occurred at every level of the urban system and contributed greatly to the employment growths of free standing cities, small and medium-sized towns in rural areas and towns within metropolitan city regions;

(v) within the service sector there were pronounced differences between services, with employment growth in the education and health services figuring prominently in the late 1960s and early 1970s, to be replaced by banking and business services in the late 1970s and early 1980s. This latter growth was not confined to South East England, but it was there that it made a substantial contribution to total employment change; and

(vi) finally, there were important shifts in employment by size of establishment; employment in large establishments declined sharply after 1970 while employment in small establishments increased as did self-employment. Once again, this was aspatially selective process; labour markets dominated by large employers tended to be in the Midlands and North, and this is where the job losses were most severe.

ES19 Our knowledge and understanding of these employment changes have been greatly advanced by the ESRC's Inner Cities Research Programme. Amongst its many findings are that, as employment growth in Britain in the 1950s turned to employment decline in the 1970s, it was the precipitous decline in manufacturing employment, especially in the largest cities, and most especially in the inner areas of these largest cities, which led the way. Their analyses show that job losses were most likely to occur in areas with high and growing proportions of (i) unemployed people; (ii) single parent families; and (iii) households without a car. These results tell us that people who lived in areas where economic and social problems were already serious were likely to see their situations made worse by further job loss.

ES20 The ICRP contained 'locality studies' of five cities (Glasgow, Newcastle, Birmingham, Bristol and London). Several conclusions about the causes of urban employment decline in the major cities were drawn from these studies. They showed, for example, the importance of inherited industrial structure, and of the effects of economic restructuring as firms closed plants or shed labour to remain competitive in the face of heightened international competition. A heavy dependence upon manufacturing industry increased the likelihood of job loss, but the sectoral structure of manufacturing mattered less than its location, with job losses concentrated in the largest cities and in the inner parts of those cities. Indigenous firms in old industrial cities showed poor performance, with low productivity due to outmoded technology and poor industrial relations. The external control of the many other firms made them vulnerable to contraction and closure, and meant that there was little demand for producer services due to the lack of senior management activities. Furthermore, the urban economies which were dominated by manufacturing industry were seemingly unsuited to the growth of new firms due to skill inflexibilities, low mobility, low levels of entrepreneurial activity and lack of innovation. However, it was not the contribution of new jobs in small firms which was the main factor which differentiated the employment changes of the five cities; it was instead the slower decline of Bristol's defence-related larger firms, in comparison with the rapid declines of the major manufacturing firms in Glasgow, Newcastle and Birmingham. Bristol also benefited from the decentralisation of office employment from London due to the high costs of land and labour in the capital. London's economic performance was poor in manufacturing but it gained from its role as the national centre of administration, management, finance, culture and tourism.

ES21 Chapter 4 also reviews other important contributions to our understanding of urban employment change, such as the 'components of change' approach (which traces the sources of all the job creations and job losses in an area), and research on the bases of employment growth in southern England (notably investment in high technology industries in the so-called 'sunbelt', and the expansion of producer services in London). But the main issues highlighted for attention are: the debate about method, summed up in the distinction between the 'location factors approach' and the 'production reorganisation (industrial restructuring) approach'; and the debate about the 'demise' of 'Fordism' and its possible replacement by 'flexible specialisation'.

ES22 Our evaluation of the research reviewed in this Chapter is:

(i) that urban manufacturing employment decline could not be satisfactorily understood using a 'location factors' approach. Instead it is necessary to relate job loss to a reorganisation of production occurring within an increasingly international economic order;

(ii) that there is a welcome trend towards research on the service sector, notably producer services and tourism;

(iii) that there is some substance to the notion of 'flexible specialisation', but that Fordist forms of mass production have not in general been replaced by the work practices of the 'flexible firm', nor are they likely to be so in the foreseeable future; and

(iv) that the image of an autonomous, private-sector, small firm based, high technology growth zone around and to the west of London must be tempered by an awareness of the international peripherality of this area, and of the degree to which this development has been linked to the defence industries and to public sector investment in transport infrastructure and research laboratories.

Chapter 5

ES23 This Chapter reviews research which traces the effects of changes in the sphere of work upon the nature of the UK urban system and of its built form character. Three themes are selected for special attention. The first concerns the past influence and likely future impacts of developments in communications technology. The main contributions to this field have come from the Centre for Urban and Regional Development Studies at the University of Newcastle. Their recent research has, amongst other things, concerned itself with the geography of the emerging 'information economy'. They claim that telecommunications, as the 'electronic highways of the future' will influence the geography of economic activity 'as much as railways did in an earlier period of profound structural change'. The determinant of the effects of the new technologies will be the patterns of access to information. The new technologies might permit wider access, thus spreading the benefits more broadly. But there are reasons for expecting the opposite. Firstly there is a regional imbalance in the distribution of 'information workers' with London and the South East leading and the northern and western regions lagging behind. Furthermore, the quality of these jobs is generally higher in London and the South East. Secondly the introduction of the new telecommunications technologies is spatially uneven, with London and a small number of major provincial cities being served first, thus endowing firms located there with a competitive advantage over firms located in other places. This advantageous position is reinforced by the costs of using the services; a firm in the South East can contact a third of all business telephones in the UK at a cost of a local call — the equivalent figure for Newcastle is 1%.

ES24 Technology also plays an important role in the second theme. This concerns the effects of the British construction industry on the nature and quality of new housing in British cities. Recent research reveals weaknesses in the UK housebuilding industry in comparison with some continental European countries. It is argued that houses in Britain are built by outmoded technology, in small numbers, on expensive land, and so are sold at very high prices. In Sweden, however, a profitable, private-sector housebuilding industry is based on a very different production system. The process is highly capital-intensive, involves production of whole sections of the house in the factory rather than on site, uses high productivity labour, and gains almost no profits from the land price increases which accompany development.

ES25 The third theme also concerns housing, but relates to the effects of employment growth on urban development in high growth regions (such as the outer South East). The new job opportunities are concentrated in service class occupations (professional, technical and managerial workers), and the local housing market becomes geared to these kinds of customers. This has the effect of making the housing far too expensive for lower paid workers and for those migrating in from other regions. Hence the recruitment problems that many employers in these kinds of places experience.

ES26 Our evaluation of the research reviewed in the Chapter is:

(i) that the failure to unpack the concept 'information' has meant that differences between information, knowledge and skills, and between information-processing and problem solving have been understated. Since the role of information and communications technology in problem solving is relatively minor, in contrast to the need for face-to-face contact which remains strong, there is a likelihood that the possibilities for decentralisation described in some of the more optimistic writings on the 'high-tech society' have been exaggerated; and

(ii) that urban change in the UK has, to an extent which is not usually acknowledged, been greatly affected by the nature of the construction industry itself — its organisation, financing, and methods of production, and its situation within the planning and land development system.

Chapter 6

ES27 This Chapter reviews the literature on the social effects of economic restructuring, both at a general level and at the level of specific localities. A large volume of ESRC-funded research has been carried out on this subject since the early 1980s notably through the 'Changing Urban and Regional System' and 'Social Change and Economic Life' Initiatives. The CURS programme attempts to explore the interaction of global restructuring processes and local social structures in the production of specific urban and regional outcomes (such as job losses or changes in political culture). Several key themes in locality change were identified by the CURS research:

(i) those which relate to the restructuring process, notably the internationalisation of the economy, the trend towards flexibility and the feminisation of the workforce;

(ii) the trend towards privatisation, both in the housing market and as a general phenomenon;

(iii) political change, not just as reflected in election results, but for example in the shift of power away from the blue collar unions towards the white collar ones;

(iv) social polarisation, especially associated with the growth of the service class;

(v) local cultures, which vary considerably between the case studies; and

(vi) local effectivity.

This last idea was given considerable prominence in the CURS work. It claims that all localities contain the capacity to become 'proactive', that is, for the inhabitants to take fate into their own hands and to act to shape the future of their locality. It is people organising themselves around locality itself as a base. The SCEL Initative was more concerned with work attitudes than CURS, and much less interested in the ways in which the economic, the social and the political connect (or do not connect) at the level of the individual locality.

ES28 Research on the social effects of recession have tended to focus on the experiences of unemployed men and the members of their households. It was found, for example, that former steelworkers tended to have 'chequered work histories' after redundancy, in which spells of employment were mixed with unemployment, self-employment and retraining. Related research has shown that economic restructuring (despite earlier expectations to the contrary) has not led to a gender role reversal within the household. Traditional gender ideology remains a strong force and a move towards unemployed men carrying out 'women's work' was resisted by both partners.

ES29 Finally, it had been thought likely that recession would lead to an expansion of the 'informal sector', as those people facing the loss of a wage searched for new sources of income in the hidden economy outside formal employment. Once again, however, this seemingly reasonable expectation was not matched by the facts. It was found that the ability of people to engage in the informal economy was closely related to their position in the formal economy. Those with jobs have the resources and contacts which permit them to add to their incomes by non-formal means. This results in a polarisation of households between those with jobs and those without.

ES30 Our evaluation of the research reviewed in this Chapter is:

(i) that certain conceptual problems with locality research, notably in connection with the idea of 'local pro-activity' have yet to be resolved;

(ii) that despite this, our understanding of the relationships between economic restructuring and social change as they are played out in specific localities is in the process of being dramatically improved as a result of the CURS and SCEL Initiatives;

(iii) that economic restructuring has brought about major social changes in different parts of the UK. However, different firms, even within the same sector, will choose different restructuring strategies, resulting in a great variety of local effects, and it is impossible to read off local class structures and local politics from the economic base of an area;

(iv) that the current emphasis on the significance of the household is fully justified, but that the category 'household', and relationships within the household, are as yet insufficiently problematised; and

(v) that at one level economic restructuring has different implications for different classes, genders and races; but at another level, class structures, gender relations and race relations may influence the way in which restructuring takes place (see Chapter 9 below).

Chapter 7

ES31 This Chapter examines the diverse literature on urban social change in the UK. It considers aspects of gender, race, politics, culture, social class and consumption. Many broad social changes have a major significance for specific places due to the concentration there of particular social groups. The ageing of the population is a good example. Recent research emphasises the different resource situations of people at different stages of the family life cycle. Elderly single-person households score very low on all three bases of material comfort (access to paid employment, net disposable income, and ownership of significant assets such as house, car, central heating etc.). This makes it likely that those areas which have a high and growing proportion of such households (for example, many inner city areas) will be areas of poverty and need. Similar arguments are advanced for other major socio-demographic changes. Much research effort is now being directed to the analysis of the recent growth of the service class of professional, technical and managerial employees, and to the characteristics of the places which have been most affected by this growth. During the same period there was a rapid decline in male manual work, so that by the early 1980s the proportion of all men of working class origin who were themselves employed in manual wage-earning jobs had fallen to about 40%. This has major implications for the social structures of northern industrial cities.

ES32 One of the most significant conceptual shifts in urban and regional studies in the past decade has been the 'rediscovery of consumption', after a time when the whole weight of theoretical enquiry and empirical research had been placed upon production. In part, this shift came about through the persistence of those who drew inspiration from the Weberian branch of political economy at a time when writers from the Marxist branch were at their most influential. But it also came from Marxist forms of analysis via the notion of 'collective consumption' developed by the French school of urban sociology. Perhaps because of this, studies of the urban dimension of consumption have tended to focus heavily on the consumption of services provided totally or to a significant extent by the public sector (such as health, education, transport, housing and social security).

ES33 Studies of social segregation, in which social class, generational and ethnic differences are typically reflected in distinctive patterns of spatial separation, have constituted a major theme in urban research for a long time. A related but more recent focus of research on UK cities has been into the 'roots of urban unrest' following the riots of 1981 and 1985. The dominant view is that while poor relationships between the police and young male Afro-Caribbeans was the trigger for the rioting, the underlying causes were to be found in the social deprivation, racial discrimination, poor housing, high unemployment, political exclusion and powerlessness experienced by many of those living in the riot-torn areas.

ES34 The recent period has seen a sudden increase in the social analysis of urban crime. This shows that, despite the caveats about the social construction of criminality and the serious inadequacy of police statistics on crime, the high incidence of criminal behaviour is a major problem for inner city residents. But an additional problem is the fear of crime, with perceptions of risk often bearing little relationship with the reality of that risk. This fear is fed by media coverage, which is then combined with rumour and folk wisdom to produce 'danger maps' of the inner city (with boundaries which are often drawn along racial lines).

ES35 Studies of socio-political change in Britain have been dominated by the debate over the class-dealignment thesis, that is the tendency for people to cease to vote for the party which traditionally represented the interests of the class to which they belong. Recent research shows that this dealignment does occur in so far as there is a tendency for a spatial polarisation of party vote. Northern and western cities are supporting the Labour Party, and southern cities the Conservatives, to a greater extent than their class structures would indicate. This is interpreted as evidence that a strong 'neighbourhood effect' has come to affect people's voting behaviours.

ES36 Finally, research on central-local relations has identified sharp changes in direction over the last twenty years, with the 1980s witnessing attempts by central government to control, both financially and politically, the activities of local authorities. This trend towards a domination of the affairs of the local authorities by central government was contested, and the course of this confrontation has attracted considerable research interest.

ES37 Our evaluation of the research reviewed in this Chapter is:

(i) that, while it is true that many recent changes have served to mask the differences between social classes (for example, separation of ownership from control, wider share-ownership and high levels of working class home ownership), we endorse the view that social class retains its salience as a determinant of opportunities, interests, values and behaviour, and that a key feature of urban change in the recent period has been the differential presence and uneven growth of the service class;

(ii) that this is not to deny the importance of consumption sector cleavages. However, despite the current emphasis to the contrary, the division between the public and the private spheres is probably as significant in the sphere of production as in that of consumption (for example, the key role of public sector unions in struggles over pay and working conditions). Housing tenure plays an important role in shaping political behaviour at certain times and in certain places, but this is a far cry from claiming that consumption cleavage has replaced class as the basis for voting;

(iii) that, in addition to class and consumption cleavage, there are other major bases for the formation of social structures in British cities, notably gender, age and 'race'. Gender relations have been intensively studied in the workplace, but relations outside the workplace remain relatively unexplored. There is a welcome re-emergence of research interest in the life cycle, and research on 'race' relations in British cities is rightly turning towards the social construction and use of racial categories; and

(iv) that ethnographic research has the potential to reveal the plurality of cultures which coexist in our cities and regions, and which help to explain diferences in response to national economic and political events. We need to know a lot more about community level social and cultural processes if we are to explain notable socio-political events such as periodic outbursts of 'popular violence' in inner cities, or the spatial polarisation of party support.

Chapter 8

ES38 This Chapter reviews research on the manner and degree to which social changes (such as the growth of the service class), politics and policies influence patterns of urban land use and built form change in UK cities. Firstly, it can be shown that social change is bringing about major changes in the physical appearance and spatial structure of British cities. A good example is the 'gentrification' — a process in which long-established manual working class communities in inner city areas come to be replaced by young middle-class owner occupiers. The newcomers modernise the buildings and set in motion changes which alter the character of the neighbourhood. Some writers link these changes to the notion of postmodernism — the inner city is seen as culturally pluralist, architecturally varied, a disorganised mixture of lifestyles and environments, in sharp contrast for example to the 'modernism' of the suburban council estate.

ES39 Gentrification transformed certain inner city areas as often as not despite the planner's wishes to maintain the social continuity of these communities. But planned landscapes are a distinctive and significant feature of 1980s Britain, and the land use planner has affected urban change through development control, new and expanded towns, the location of major infrastructure investments, green belt policies and containment, and so on. Recent research has focused attention on planning as it is actually practised, as planners mediate urban change through negotiations with developers, local authorities and residents in different urban environments (such as the city centre, the inner city and the urban fringe). The evidence suggests that it is in the inner city that planning is least effective in determining outcomes. Here its actions are limited by the fact that these areas have dwindling resources, are overdependent on the public sector, and because planners face almost insuperable problems of co-ordination between public sector agencies in what is often a highly charged political environment.

ES40 Research which evaluates government policies affecting the housing and built form character of UK cities is largely critical of the changes which have been put in place since 1979. The exception, perhaps, is the housing improvement programme in Glasgow where a conjunction of positive attitudes and actions on the part of the SDA, housing associations, local authorities and residents has helped to produce a significant rejuvenation of housing stock and an improvement in the development prospects of Glasgow's inner city areas.

ES41 Our evaluation of the research reviewed in this Chapter is:

(i) that new gender relations and the growth of the service class have produced significant land use and built form changes in inner city neighbourhoods, notably through the process of gentrification. However, more needs to be known about individual housing and labour market careers before gentrification can be viewed as a permanent feature of UK urban change. We would argue that it is not sufficient to assume that the labour market impacts on a passive housing market, rather it is quite possible that gentrification is itself affecting the nature of inner city labour markets and the kinds of investments occurring there; and

(ii) that as far as the role of state intervention in shaping urban built form is concerned, we would suggest that a fully considered assessment of the ways in which shifts in public policy and reductions in planning authority have affected development outcomes has yet to appear.

Chapter 9

ES42 This final Chapter reviews research which raises some central questions about urban change in the UK in the recent period. It explores the ways in which the economic performance of cities and regions has been affected by social and cultural factors, and by the state (both central and local) through urban and regional development policies. On the latter theme research shows that differential urban change results not only from policies designed to promote development in particular cities or parts of cities, but also from national policies intended to apply to the whole country. An example of this is financial assistance to small firms where take up was higher in the south and east of England than in the regions of the north and west. In this way the policy for supporting small firms, though national in scope, boosts economic activity in regions which are already privileged, and therefore runs counter to the purposes of regional policy.

ES43 Most research on the effects of government regional policy comes to the conclusion that this policy was highly successful during the period from the early-mid 1960s to the mid-1970s. One study claims that as many as 450,000 new jobs were created in the assisted areas by manufacturing investment diverted there through controls on land development for industry in the South East, investment incentives, and an employment subsidy paid to firms in the north and west.

ES44 Similar evaluative studies have been carried out on the government's Enterprise Zone policy, and on the Urban Development Corporations. Certain key issues seem to arise repeatedly in these evaluation exercises. To what extent do these initiatives create investments which would not otherwise have occurred (the additionality problem)? To what extent do the new investments serve to undermine existing production in the area (the replacement problem)? And above all, who are the beneficiaries of the new investments? Are the new jobs and houses going to the residents of the inner city, or are the jobs being taken by commuters from the suburbs and the houses by in-coming gentrifiers (the targeting problem)?

ES45 Local authority economic development initiatives have also received considerable research attention. In particular, there has been a lot of interest in 'local socialism', the attempt by a small number of radical local authorities to institute 'alternative economic strategies' to promote local economic development. While many of these interventions were novel in the way in which they prioritised the interests of workers rather than owners, the benefits were insignificant in relation to the size of the unemployment and poverty problems that these local authorities were facing. It was, as one commentator put it, like 'trying to empty the ocean with a teaspoon'.

ES46 State intervention is by no means the only way in which the social and the political can affect the pace and nature of urban economic change. One of the most influential conceptual developments in urban and regional research during the recent period has been the idea that one can visualise the changing social and economic geography of the UK in terms of 'spatial divisions of labour'. More specifically, it is argued that the dominant spatial division of labour in the early post war period was 'regional sectoral specialisation', but that this came to be overlain and partially replaced during the 1960s and 70s by a new or 'hierarchical' spatial division of labour, in which the differences between places were to be found not so much in what goods or services were produced there but in terms of the role that the labour force played in the overall production process (for example, management in London, research and development. in the 'sunbelt', and routine production in the north and west). A key element in this approach is that the changes which occur in particular places are guided by the social, political and cultural outcomes of the roles that those places had played in previous spatial divisions of labour.

ES47 Our evaluation of the research reviewed in this Chapter is:

(i) that using only industrial structure and policy to analyse the impact of regional policy is inadequate since the differential performance of cities and regions could in fact be caused by any number of processes (for example, economic restructuring and the search for cheap and manageable labour);

(ii) that variation in local private and public sector institutions, and in local political cultures were important in mediating the effects of national policies in local areas; and

(iii) that when it comes to the role of social structures in influencing economic performance, research should continue to draw upon the spatial divisions of labour approach, and should stress the importance of the 'combination of layers' of past rounds of accumulation in affecting present patterns of urban and regional economic development.

ES48 On balance, the quality and quantity of recent research on patterns and processes of urban change in the UK is very impressive. The interminable methodological and philosophical debates of the 1970s have largely disappeared to be replaced by intelligent and thoughtful empirical analyses of contemporary changes. These analyses are usually based upon large datasets derived from published statistics or from interview surveys, but the manner in which these statistics are used is less positivistic, more practical, less sophisticated perhaps, but much more useful. As for perspective, the boundaries between disciplines and approaches seem, at last, to be coming down. Most researchers adopt a political economy perspective, not usually in the narrow sense of a Marxist political economy, but in order to be able to bring together the economic and the social, with the spatial and the historical. But if these are the strengths of the recent literature, there are also some weaknesses. Analyses of urban change by economists trail well behind those of the sociologists and the geographers. Also, our knowledge of the physical structures of our cities, and of the ways in which those physical structures impact on social relations and economic development remains woefully limited. These shortcomings are serious and should be remedied, but they detract little from our main conclusion which is that this has been an extremely productive field of research in the recent period.

INTRODUCTION

The structure of the report

0.1 The patterns of urban change in the UK are complex and the processes which produce them are many and varied. Because of this, the task of reviewing the very extensive literature on the subject was sure to be a formidable one. During our work, however, two further characteristics of the literature emerged. The first was that the amount and quality of the empirical research available on urban change varied enormously from one aspect of the subject to another. The second was that the theoretical perspectives drawn upon by the researchers were quite often incompatible; this meant that there were important differences between the studies in what was assumed to be already known and agreed upon. The result of this unevenness and incompatibility is a body of literature which is characterised as much by disjuncture as by complementarity. Our dilemma was how to express these inconsistencies and complexities in an efficient manner, without imposing a theoretical framework of our own — a framework which might itself give a falsely consistent view of the subject.

0.2 Our attempt to solve this problem involved two steps. The first was to make decisions as to what particular changes might be included in the notion of 'urban change' referred to in the title of the report. It was decided that such changes could be grouped under three headings:

(a) those that concern the town or city as a material artefact. This primarily refers to **urban land use and built form**, but it also includes the city as an object, set within the physical context of its region and of the national territory. Thus the kinds of changes which are of interest are those that involve additions to, subtrac-

tions from, and transformations in, the built up area of the city, together with **urban growth and decline** (as measured by population change) studied within the context of a changing settlement system;

(b) those that concern the town or city as a place of **work and employment**. Thus the kinds of changes which are of interest here are the job losses in many midland and northern industrial cities brought about by the economic restructuring of the UK economy, job gains in the producer services sector such as have occurred in London, the increase in part-time employment for women, and changes in management-labour relations; and

(c) those that concern the town or city as a place where people make their homes, develop friendships, raise children, spend their leisure time, form their political opinions, and engage in organised social activities. Thus the kinds of changes which are of interest are those that reflect the ability, or the intention, of people to engage fully in these **social, cultural and political activities.** Such changes are the emergence of an 'urban underclass', the increasing levels of car and home ownership, the decreasing significance of nuclear family households, and the centralisation of political power.

0.3 The second step towards providing a framework which was simple, consistent and yet relatively neutral theoretically, was now fairly straightforward. Many important processes and relationships of urban change can be researched within the categories listed above. For example, the decentralisation of shopping facilities can be explained in terms of land use processes and the redistribution of the urban population. But many of the most interesting and challenging ideas about how and why towns and cities have changed in the recent period involve claims about the ways in which one of the dimensions listed above impacts upon one of the other dimensions. Thus Fothergill and Gudgin, for example, claim that the urban environment, through its rigidities of land use and built form (often experienced by firms as a lack of space for site redevelopment) has adversely affected manufacturing employment change in the major cities of Britain during the recent period and has thus helped to bring about the urban-rural shift in manufacturing employment.

0.4   To this end each piece of empirical research was classified EITHER under one of the three main headings:

(a) urban settlement and built form;

(b) work and employment; or

(c) social relations;

OR placed in one of the six categories which link these dimensions or elements of urban change.

Figure 1 illustrates the nine categories of research which result from this. Our review of the literature on patterns and processes of urban change in the UK is thus organised around these nine categories with each one having a separate Chapter in the report. We do not intend to suggest by this that there is an equality of importance of each of the categories, nor that every piece of research falls neatly into just one category. However, we do feel that this scheme allows us to encompass all the really important research initiatives in this field, while at the same time focussing attention on the nature of the causal claims which they make.

0.5   Thus the structure of the Report is as follows:

a. Urban settlement and built form

Chapter 1. Changing patterns of population and land use in the UK urban system (spatial change).

Chapter 2. The role of location, land use and built form in urban economic performance (space and economy).

Chapter 3. The role of housing and built form in shaping social relations (space and society.)

b. Work and employment

Chapter 4. Urban employment change in the UK: patterns and processes (economic development).

Chapter 5. The influence of economic and technological change on the urban system and on urban built form (economy and space).

Chapter 6. The impact on employment change on social life (economy and society).

c. Social relations

Chapter 7. Politics, culture and the household; patterns and processes of social change in UK cities and regions (social change).

Chapter 8. The influence of social change, politics and policy on urban built form (society and space).

Chapter 9. The role of local social relations, politics and culture in shaping urban economic performance (society and economy).

0.6   The 3000 or so references gained from a wide search of the literature were then divided between these Chapters, and between their subdivisions (listed in the Contents). From this extensive bibliography we selected just 60 titles for detailed attention. They were chosen on the basis of their relevance to an understanding of urban change in the UK, and to show the range of research styles and perspectives. Summaries of their contents are integrated into the text of the report. Each Chapter of the report is divided into three sections: in the first, the main issues are raised; in the second, the major contributions are discussed; and in the third, we evaluate the literature.

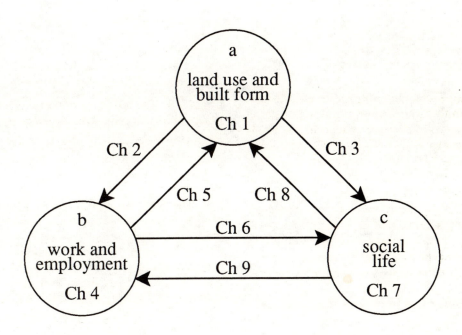

Figure 1 : The Structure of the Report

CHAPTER 1

Changing patterns of population and land use in the UK urban system

counter-urbanisation.

1.1 This Chapter reviews research on the growth and decline of towns and cities in the UK (as measured by their changing population sizes), and on changes in urban land use and built form. Three groups of processes can be identified. Firstly, certain demographic changes bring about an altered spatial distribution of the population. These changes are customarily divided into: (i) natural increase, where the differences between places arise from variations in fertility and mortality rates, and in the age compositions of their populations; and (ii) net migration. Particular attention has been paid to the recent patterns and processes of inter-regional and intra-regional migration since these have been of paramount importance in determining population redistribution. Secondly, processes of land and property development have transformed the land use and built form characteristics of UK towns and cities. Land has been converted from non-urban to urban use; office buildings, shopping centres and industrial estates have been built; and land values have changed as accessibility patterns have been modified by the construction of new transport facilities (such as the M25 motorway around London). Thirdly, and more specifically, the spatial structure of the housing stock has been altered by new house building and demolitions, and by the incidence of repairs and renovations.

Issues

1.2 A number of important empirical questions arise with respect to these changes. What has happened to the UK urban system since 1970? In settlements of what size and location have the populations increased or decreased most markedly? Where did these changes occur? And how did they come about? What has happened to the city itself as a system? How has the inner city fared? Where did the major changes in population and land use occur? How did these changes come about?

1.3 Attempts to deal with these questions, mostly by geographers and economists, have tended to cluster around two broad issues:

(i) can it be argued that population redistribution patterns changed fundamentally from an urbanisation form to a counterurbanisation one in the late 1960s/early 1970s? The 1981 census results seemed to confirm that population growth in the 1970s was typically to be found in small and medium-sized settlements often located well outside the commuting zones of the largest cities and industrial conurbations, whose populations were without exception declining. Should this be interpreted as an important new departure or is it, as some have claimed, nothing more than the further development of previous trends, or as others have claimed, only a temporary phase in population redistribution? And

(ii) are the towns and cities of the UK passing through stages of urban development in a manner conformable with an urban life-cycle model (see 1.16 below)? While accepting that each city's development is to some extent unique, can one recognise certain regularities in the way that urban areas grow and decline through time and over space? More specifically, should we expect to see a sequence which runs from urbanisation, through suburbanisation and de-urbanisation to re-urbanisation, as Klaassen and van den Berg would have us believe? There would be major planning implications if this were so, because it would mean that we would have to expect a re-urbanisation of most of Britain's major cities during the 1990s.

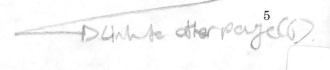

Contributions

1.4 Academic research on the changing patterns of population and land use in the UK urban system can be grouped under four headings:

(i) those that describe the demographic and economic aspects of urban development in the UK in a general, often historical, manner, sometimes focussing on the evolution of specific cities or regions;

(ii) those that describe and account for the changing patterns of inter- and intra-regional migration;

(iii) those that attempt to interpret the patterns of urban growth and decline within an urban systems framework and/or with the help of standard economic analysis; and

(iv) those that describe and account for the changing patterns of urban land use and built form, notably the location and relocation of offices, shops and factories; and the spatial aspects of changes in the UK housing stock.

1(i) General and historical studies of the demographic and economic aspects of urban development in the UK

1.5 Many studies have attempted to synthesise the broad features of urban change in the UK in the recent period. They point to the following main elements:

(i) a decline in population and employment in the largest cities, and a tendency for population and employment growth to be concentrated in free-standing cities, and in the small and medium-sized towns located in rural and semi-urban areas;

(ii) a bias towards growth in the southern part of the country and decline in the north (independently of city-size effects); and

(iii) a tendency for growth to be concentrated in suburban and peri-urban areas, and decline to be concentrated in the inner city.

1.6 A notable recent research development, attracting media, business and government interest, is the fashion for 'rating places' (**Champion and Green** 1988). The aim of Champion and Green's study is to reveal the patterns of growth and decline in 1980s Britain through indices based upon labour and housing market variables and on population change. Their 'static' index measures the level of prosperity in the mid-1980s and uses unemployment rate, duration of unemployment, employment in producer services and high technology industries, economic activity rate, and house prices. Their 'change' index measures 'local dynamism' in the early-mid 1980s and uses changes in unemployment

rate, changes in total employment, change in employment in producer services and high technology industries, population change, and change in house prices. The areal units used in the analysis are the 280 Local Labour Market Areas developed at the Centre for Urban and Regional Development Studies at the University of Newcastle (CURDS).

Similar to comps in OZ?

1.7 The main results of this research are firstly, that there is a clear north/south divide; both levels of prosperity and dynamism are higher in the south than in the north. There is also evidence that this division has become greater during the recent period, partly because of the marked improvement in the position of London in the early-mid 1980s. Secondly, that there is a major arc of growth and prosperity around and to the west of London. Thirdly, that a few places north and west of the Severn/Wash line show both prosperity and growth (notably the Richmond area in North Yorkshire). Fourthly, that all of the main cities of northern and western Britain perform below the median on both the static and the change indices. And finally, that the distributions of the static index (level of prosperity) and the change index (dynamism) are positively correlated, which means that the prosperous places are doing even better and the areas lacking in prosperity are doing even worse. One might expect such differences to provoke sizeable flows of migrants from the north and west towards the south and east, but as we shall see below, there are serious barriers to such migration.

1(ii) Population redistribution: migration and the UK urban system

1.8 For many researchers urban change is synonymous with population redistribution, and a considerable literature on recent patterns of population change in the UK has resulted. Most of these studies focus attention upon inter- and intra-regional migration, and many are concerned with the relationship between net migration and settlement size.

Counter-urbanisation.

1.9 Following the urbanisation and suburbanisation of the previous decades, the 1970s can be characterised as a decade of counterurbanisation. The term 'counterurbanisation' is controversial. Firstly, many have difficulty in distinguishing it from suburbanisation; secondly, some feel that it implies that the new built form in non-metropolitan regions was not urban in character, and finally, others equate the term with an inference that the trends were caused by anti-urbanism. However, counterurbanisation (conceptualised as 'decentralised urbanisation', and measured as an inverse relationship between net migration rate and settlement size, that is, the larger the settlement the greater the net migration loss, the smaller the settlement the greater the gain, at the functional urban region level) is now accepted as being a property of population redistribution patterns in most western industrial countries in the 1970s, and analyses of migration patterns in the UK confirm that this country was no exception to the rule.

1.10 An important empirical study of these population redistribution trends of the 1970s was carried out over the period 1984–86 by Halcrow Fox and Associates and Birkbeck College for the Department of the Environment (hereafter DoE) (**Halcrow Fox** 1986). The project had two special features which mark it out from those conducted by the Centre for Urban and Regional Development Studies (CURDS) at the University of Newcastle. The first was that it was only concerned with the 957 small and medium-sized settlements (SAMS), that is, places with populations of between 5,000 and 100,000 in 1981. The second was that the settlements were defined physically, as areas of 'irreversibly urban' land use, rather than administratively or in terms of labour market areas. Unfortunately, the study included only the SAMS in England, and the data set did not include the results of the 10% sample section of the census. Nevertheless, the results are intriguing. Between 1971 and 1981 the population of SAMS urban areas increased by 5.9% at a time when the total population grew by only 0.7%, SAMS in the south grew faster than those in the north, and smaller SAMS faster than larger ones. Above all, there was a strong tendency for free-standing SAMS to grow rapidly, whatever size they were and in whichever region they were located, and this growth was associated with increases in non-manual and service employment, and with growth in owner-occupation and car ownership. The cluster analysis revealed that the highest population growth rates were to be found in 'Growth Commuter Areas with Mixed Employment', in 'Rural and Free-Standing Towns', in 'Growth through Manufacturing Prosperity' areas and in Milton Keynes (which had a cluster to itself!). The study also tested ideas about the effects of public policy; it found evidence that New and Expanded Towns grew faster than the average, that those located in the Green Belts grew more slowly, but that location close to a motorway did not in general provide the impetus to growth that one might expect.

1.11 The Halcrow Fox/Birkbeck study demonstrated the usefulness of the urban areas data, which can be seen as complementary to the functional urban region data (that is, regions defined on the basis of journey-to-work movements) used by other groups; it demonstrated the importance of growth in SAMS which were not part of the commuter areas of large cities, and especially the growth of small towns in the East Anglian, South Western and outer South Eastern regions. Despite its attempt to model urban growth it should be seen more as a descriptive survey of the variables associated with the population growths of small and medium-sized urban areas than as a contribution to our theoretical understanding of the processes of change.

1.12 Census data tell us a great deal about migration in 1970–1 and 1980–1, but very little about what happened either between these dates or since 1981. Studies which have drawn upon alternative sources of information have revealed other important aspects of population redistribution. Several researchers have used the National Health Central Register (NHSCR) data to study gross inter-regional migration flows at the regional and county levels, and the Office of Population Censuses and Surveys (OPCS) mid-year estimates can also be used to study net migration by local authority areas on an annual basis.

1.13 The NHSCR data has been used particularly successfully by the Leeds University team in their work on describing and forecasting migration trends. In a conference paper dated April, 1988, **Stillwell, Boden and Rees** trace internal migration flows in the UK at a number of spatial scales over the period 1975–6 to 1985–6. They show that the periphery (Wales, Scotland, Northern Ireland and the Northern region) went from being a net gainer by internal migration in 1975–6 to being a net loser thereafter; the industrial heartland (North West, West Midlands and Yorkshire and Humberside regions) lost throughout the period; and the southern half of England gained throughout the period, but that these gains were partly offset, especially during the late 1970s, by the losses incurred by Greater London. At the metropolitan level they show that while all metropolitan regions lost over this period, South Yorkshire did particularly badly, and that Greater London improved its position in the early-mid 1980s only to fall back again by 1986. Analysis at the level of the Family Practitioner Committee Areas reveals that this improvement in London's position was largely due to the reduced losses (and even some gains) in the inner London Boroughs. It also shows the persistently high net losses of certain major cities such as Liverpool, the persistently high net gains of many south coast counties (especially East and West Sussex, Dorset and the Isle of Wight, and Cornwall), and the areas where shifts were occurring, such as the deteriorating position of Cleveland. They then investigate gross migration flows to see if there were changes in the 'level, generation, attraction, and distribution' components of the flows. From this analysis it was possible to assert, for example, that London's improvement was largely due to lower out-migration, and that as a destination, it was increasingly attractive to migrants from outside the South. Stillwell, Boden and Rees conclude that counterurbanisation was still evident in the south, but was less apparent in the north, and that movement away from the north continued during the 1980s, resulting in a widening of the migration gap between north and south.

1.14 Studies of this kind show that the peak period for counterurbanisation in the UK was during the last years of the 1960s and the first years of the 1970s; since then the rates of loss of the major cities, especially London, have declined. The improved position of London and the poorer performance of small towns and rural areas in northern Britain has brought attention back to the north/south dimension of population redistribution in the UK.

1(iii) Change in UK urban system: urban economic studies

1.15 The concept of an urban system has its early origins in the theoretical work of geographers and economists such as Christaller and Losch, but it was popularised in the late 1960s by Brian Berry in his teaching and research at the University of Chicago. It has certain advantages for a study of urban change; it focuses attention on: (i) the interdependencies between places, and therefore on the importance of relative location; and (ii) on the properties of the settlement system as a whole, for example, the frequency distribution of settlements by size, rather than on the characteristics of the individual city. However, in the recent period, the research emphasis has been rather more on the specificity of places, an emphasis which is reflected in the popularity of 'locality studies'. Research couched in the language of urban systems has, in contrast, become distinctly unfashionable.

1.16 An important research theme which maintains the urban systems tradition is represented by empirical studies of the 'urban life-cycle'. This work has its origins in a study by Peter Hall and others on the 'Containment of Urban Britain'. It was bring developed by Hall and others in their studies of Western European urbanisation, but it reaches its highest degree of sophistication in further studies of urban change in Western Europe by Klaassen and van den Berg. These authors see evidence for a cyclical process of growth and decline in the patterns of post-war urban development. They point out that there are clear patterns of urban development over space, and great similarities between cities in the paths of their urban development over time. The stages of development in this urban life-cycle approach are shown in Figure 2.

1.17 An assertive use of the urban life-cycle approach for the functional urban regions of the European Community has been made by Paul Cheshire and his team at the University of Reading (**Cheshire and Hay** 1988). Both the strengths and the weaknesses of the approach are revealed in this particular study. In Table 7.1 of their book they present data for all the functional urban regions in the European Community with populations of over 330,000 for the periods 1950–60,

1960–70, 1970–75 and 1975–80, classified by location and by stage of development. A clear pattern emerges; the peak frequencies move from stages involving concentration (8, 1, 2 and 3) in the 1950s, towards those of decentralisation in the late 1970s (2, 3, 4 and 5), and there is a clear tendency for the northern countries to lead and the southern countries to lag.

1.18 The analyses by the Reading team are wide-ranging, and the use of the urban life-cycle model forms only a small part of their work. Their project, funded by the European Community (EC) and begun in 1983, consists of a comparative study of urban change in the member countries of the EC. Data for 344 functional urban regions were analysed, and more detailed studies were carried out for 50 cities from this list. Four categories of city were identified:

(i) the growing city in a low income region;

(ii) healthy growing cities (an example in Britain is Norwich);

(iii) cities declining in population without major urban problems (according to Cheshire and Hay this includes London); and

(iv) declining cities with problems.

This last category includes most of the largest cities in Britain. Multiple regression techniques are used to examine the relationships between urban population growth/decline and a number of contextual economic and environmental variables.

1.19 In their explanations of the changes the Reading team are largely concerned to reassert the importance of economic 'factors' in the urban growth process. In particular, there is great emphasis on the role of improvements in transportation technology, and implications of a shift away from the use of railways and seaports towards a use of motorways and airports. With economic prosperity comes suburbanisation of the major cities, which with deindustrialisation leads to inner city decay, followed in some cases by the recentralisation of the middle class, as in Glasgow. Industrial structure is also important with cities dependent on a large plant manufacturing industry tending to decline, while those involved in the service sectors, including producer services and tourism tend to grow. At the same time those cities located close to the core area of the enlarged European economic space fare better than those which are now rendered peripheral (compare Felixstowe and Dover with Liverpool).

1(iv) Land use and built form changes: offices, shops and factories; residential land use changes; economic studies of housing

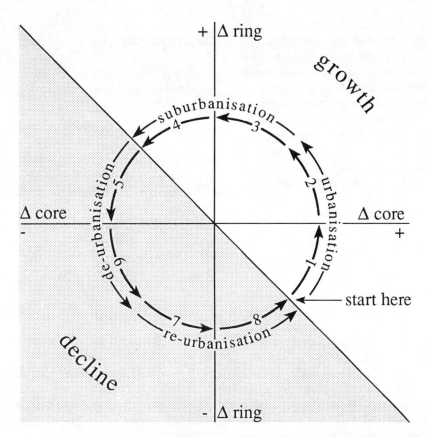

+ |Δ ring

growth

suburbanisation

4 3

urbanisation

de-urbanisation

5 2

Δ core
-

Δ core
+

6 1

start here

7 8

re-urbanisation

decline

- |Δ ring

Figure 2 : The Urban Life-Cycle Model

PHOTOCOPY.

1.20 Despite the rhetoric of the 'vanishing country-side', the general picture is one of a relative stability of land use in the post-war period, brought about partly by the continuity of agricultural production but bolstered by the planning restrictions placed upon the physical expansion of urban areas. However, this picture of the recent past must be qualified to take account of the significant suburbanisation which was permitted. Land conversion for housing and other urban land uses was fairly rapid in the 1950s, 1960s and early 1970s, but slowed down after this due to the decline of house building on greenfield sites. There are, in addition, important local and regional exceptions to this broad stability of land use. The areas beyond the London metropolitan Green Belt, notably the Thames Valley — M4 corridor and the areas affected by the other radial routes around London have been particularly affected by new urban development (see Section 5.1 below), and sizeable conversions of agricultural land to urban land uses have accompanied motorway construction and the further expansion of the New and Expanded Towns, especially Milton Keynes. *TRANSPORT*

1.21 Recession may have reduced the overall pressure on agricultural land, but it also resulted in important land use changes within urban areas. Above all, factory closures, and the decline and restructuring of seaports and railways added to the considerable amounts of derelict land already present in many industrial cities in the Midlands and North of England, and in Central Scotland, South Wales and Northern Ireland.

1.22 Studies of land use changes are far from sufficient to provide us with a rounded picture of these developments, although both losses of agricultural land and inner city waste land have attracted polemical tracts. The Wye College team have made good use of the poor data available, and the DoE now monitors land use changes in a more systematic way, but there are few if any authoritative and up-to-date accounts of land use change in the UK.

1.23 Rather more encouraging are the specialised studies of vacant urban land, especially derelict land in the inner city. A good example of such research is the paper by **Adams, Baum and MacGregor** (1985) on the influence of valuation practices on the price of inner city land, and hence its attractiveness to new investment. Drawing upon evidence for Manchester, they argue that these practices prevent vacant land prices from falling even when such land is in over-supply. The possible reasons for this are all related to the importance of the public sector in inner area land transactions, and are firstly, 'that the statutory rules of valuation within the compensation code produces a higher sum paid in compensation on compulsory acquisition than would be achieved in an open market sale. This raises seller's expectations and sets a floor below which prices in the open market do not fall'. The authors found too little compulsory purchase to prove this point, but they thought it possible that the prospect of paying high sums in compensation may encourage local authorities to reach voluntary settlements which exceed market prices.

- Land use change.
- Recession.
- derelict land.

9

1.24 The second reason is 'that the prices paid by public authorities on acquisition in the open market raise seller's expectations and (again) set a floor below which market prices will not fall'. Adams, Bauer and MacGregor found that public bodies were active as purchasers of land, that they were thought to pay more than private buyers, and that this encouraged vendors to hold out for a public sector acquisition. The third possible reason is 'that conventional valuation practices maintain high land prices'. This is likely when, as in local authority practice, land price is calculated using past and non-local comparisons. But private sector developers tend to see land price as a residual element; that is, they work out what is the maximum they are prepared to pay for the land having already costed the project and allowed for their profit. The comparative method tends on the evidence to produce higher prices than the residual method. The authors conclude by saying that the infrequency of transactions in the inner city and the uniqueness of each site makes the valuation process fraught with difficulty, and even prompts the question as to whether or not there is a land 'market' in the inner city. In these circumstances valuation tends to place undue emphasis on the most favourable recent transaction. 'As a result asking prices for vacant land on the market are often substantially in excess of median prices actually achieved in recent transactions. Land prices in inner cities are therefore revised downwards only slowly and reluctantly in response to lack of demand or excess supply. This creates a blockage in the development process and prolongs the period of vacancy'.

1.25 The product of these land development processes is an 'urban morphology' (that is, a particular land use and built form structure). A major synthesis of research on urban morphology has recently been published by **Whitehand** (1987). Drawing examples from many western industrial countries Whitehand argues for a theory of urban built form development which combines the von Thunen/Alonso-Muth 'bid rent curve' analysis with an appreciation of the importance of building cycles. During a housebuilding slump, the physical expansion of the city will take the form of additions of low-intensity urban land uses to the outer edge of the built up area. When housebuilding picks up, a more intensive form of land use will be added to the new outer edge. In this way bands of lower intensity uses become absorbed into the built form fabric of the city inviting redevelopment opportunities at some future date. The emphasis throughout is in the longevity of urban built form, in contrast to the uses to which that built form is put, and on the way in which past structures (street layout for example) shape subsequent development.

Evaluation

1.26 Our main findings in relation to the literature reviewed in this chapter are as follows:

(i) that there is a wealth of data analysis and interpretation on patterns of urban, rural and regional population change. This establishes that a major shift in redistribution trends occurred in the late 1960s/early 1970s towards a counterurbanisation, or decentralised urbanisation, pattern of development. It also shows that this pattern became partially replaced by a new north-south division in the more recent period. However, this research tends to be long on description and short on explanation. Perhaps particularly disappointing are the studies which use multiple regression techniques to 'explain' differential urban population growth rates; these rarely penetrate the processes which underpin urban change — they are descriptions of patterns of co-variation not explanations. The implications of these trends for urban policy-makers are that development pressures seem set to continue to be greatest in the non-metropolitan areas of southern Britain, and least in the metropolitan areas of northern Britain;

(ii) that the urban life-cycle model, though descriptively interesting, contributes little to our understanding of how and why cities change. Rather, it tends to foster the view that these time/space patterns are somehow natural and immutable, impervious to policy and to political economy alike. Although the rates of net migration loss experienced by the inner cities declined in the late 1970s and early 1980s, there are no signs of the general turnround predicted by this model and implied by the term 're-urbanisation'. Such a turnround, if it were to occur, would have major significance for urban policy-making; and

(iii) that remarkably little general work has been done on changes in land use and built form. We do not have accurate information on the intra-urban, urban or regional changes in land uses, nor can we learn what changes have taken place in the stock of buildings by age or type or use. Perhaps this is because the statistics are so sparse and often of poor quality. Or is it because the questions we have concentrated upon in the recent period have not called for a better knowledge of these changes? For whatever reason, we seem to be remarkably ignorant about the physical structures of the cities within which we live out our lives. This is something which should be addressed in the planning of the Government's statistical activities and in deciding future research priorities.

CHAPTER 2

The role of location, land use and built form in urban economic performance

2.1 This Chapter reviews research which claims that it is the physical structure of an area, (for example, its land use and built form characteristics), or its relative location (for example, with respect to some major environmental feature), which determines that area's economic performance. Also included is work based upon the idea that the relationship between people and their material environments (house/home, neighbourhood/community, city/home-town), for example through housing tenure, can act as a constraint upon economic restructuring, and lead to low growth and unemployment.

Issues

2.2 Among the many issues which can be placed under this heading the following have been the main ones to have received attention during the recent period:

(i) can high unemployment be explained in part as resulting from low geographical mobility, which in turn comes about from rigidities in the population/housing relationship (notably in public sector housing and in the form of rent controls)?

(ii) are UK towns and cities 'unfairly structured' so that certain groups, due to their residential location, are unable to take advantage of the jobs, shopping facilities, leisure amenities etc, to which other groups have easy access? In particular, does urban built form restrict womens' access to paid employment?

(iii) what role does infrastructure investment play in urban employment change, and how do the characteristics of the physical environment affect the

economic performance of cities? and

(iv) do rigidities in land use and built form in the major cities during the post-war period explain the urban-rural shift in manufacturing employment? More generally, what role does land play in the industrial development process? The policy implications of this issue are considerable, because if constraints on site development turn out to be crucial, then that is where state intervention is most likely to be effective.

Contributions

2(i) Housing influences on labour markets; inter-regional immobility and unemployment

2.3 The key idea in the literature reviewed in this section is that the separations between work and residence at a broad regional scale cause high levels of unemployment. In the late 1970s and 1980s the jobs have tended to be in the south of England while the homes of many of the potential holders of these jobs remain in the northern and western regions of the UK.

2.4 Theoretical approaches associated with neoclassical economics acknowledge that inequalities can appear among regions. In so far, however, as markets are allowed to work, these initial differences will be ironed out as a result of the emergence of equilibrating mechanisms. To explain the persistence of imbalances, writers in this tradition highlight the role of rigidities in the market for labour arising from the relationship between people and their housing, and from the attachment they have for their present area of residence. The central hypothesis is that unemployment is a result of insufficient geographical mobility brought about by the role of subsidised housing and unemployment benefit in enabling households to survive without seeking paid work. In areas of economic decline council housing and housing benefits are disincentives to work. If these supports were removed individuals would be forced to seek jobs elsewhere and would, moreover, be prepared to accept the lower wages on which an increase in employment depends. An example of this approach is provided by **Minford, Peel and Ashton** (1987). Minford et al. claim, on the basis of regression equations, that if mobility constraints were lifted so that the unemployed were completely inter-regionally mobile, total unemployment would fall by 500,000 and 1% would be added to the gross domestic product (see 2.17 for an evaluation of this position).

2.5 Housing market influences on the labour market are 'centre stage' as a research field at the moment, and it is not surprising that this subject forms the focus of a major research initiative financed by the Rowntree Trust now being carried out by a joint team from the Centre for Housing Studies at the University of Glasgow and CURDS at Newcastle.

2(ii) Residential structure effects on employment opportunities; urban transportation and the journey to work

2.6 The separation of work from residence is also an issue at a more local level. Each location within the city has a different level of accessibility to the job opportunities which are available in the area, but that accessibility is mediated by the personal and household circumstances of those seeking work. However, our understanding of these issues has been hampered by the tendency for studies of urban transportation to be age, class, gender and ethnicity 'blind', and to be overly concerned with the technical problems of forecasting transport (especially road transport) demand.

2.7 However, partly as a result of studies of the role of urban spatial structure in women's access to paid employment, this is beginning to change. This research has drawn attention to the fact that the form of the built environment and the spatial organisation of our cities hold different implications for men and women. Perhaps the most obvious example of this concerns building design and planning in connection with women's safety from physical assault. Less immediately obvious, however, are the ways in which urban land use and transportation might act as constraints upon women's access to paid employment, or influence the types of paid work in which women are able to participate. It is argued that far from being 'neutral', the built environment and transport structure are based on certain assumptions about gender roles within the

family, and that some of these assumptions bear a decreasing resemblance to reality.

2.8 Central to post-war principles of land use zoning was the separation of the industry and employment from housing, schools and shops. At the same time assumptions were made about the division of labour within the household between men and women. These rested on an ideal type of the nuclear family in which the man participated in full-time waged work whilst the woman remained in the home and was responsible for domestic labour. The model became one of women in the suburbs and men in the city, and is perhaps most clearly reflected in the planned new towns of the post-war period. Indeed, 'not only was this suburban environment predicated on the labour of a full-time suburban housewife, it also made it very difficult to organise the domestic economy and home life in any other way' (Mackenzie and Rose 1983).

2.9 However, this nuclear family scenario with the unproblematic separation of the public and the private, bears little relationship to modern social reality. The notion of woman as housewife has never been universally borne out, and since the Second World War has become increasingly less so. Of the 2.4 million overall increase in the British working population between 1951 and 1971, 2.2 million were women and women represented over 45% of the workforce in mid-1987. 50% of all married women are in paid employment, which is not far short of the 54% for unmarried women. With these considerations in mind **Foord and Lewis** (1984) investigated the impact of built form on female labour supplies and economic restructuring in Peterlee and East Kilbride New Towns. In the case of Peterlee one of the original aims of developing the new town was to absorb female labour in a coal mining region, this despite the fact that the town was planned along the spatially segregated lines described above. By the late 1960s the local employers were experiencing labour shortages. The methods they used to overcome these shortages reflect the constraints which physical form and transport structure were imposing on the local labour market. Employers introduced changes in working practices which would allow women to combine their dual role as domestic worker and paid employee in an environment where the two roles were physically separated; they included twilight shifts, part-time working and flexible holiday systems. In East Kilbride on the other hand, the intention had been to build up a skilled male engineering workforce. What happened, in fact, was that the town grew up around the reserves of female labour unintentionally created by the establishment of the new town, and the participation of women workers in light manufacturing, electronics and the service sector. Although different cases, the histories of Peterlee and East Kilbride show that the participation of women in the workforce was crucial to local economic growth. Physical separation of home, schools, shops and work do not make this participation easy, given women's responsibility for domestic labour.

2.10   The difficulties which women face in combining their dual role in the context of the spatial separation of land use is compounded by inequalities of mobility between men and women. Bus networks and timetables are frequently organised around the needs of the full-time worker; the services for part-time workers (almost entirely women) are often inadequate. Nor do they meet other, sometimes incredibly complicated, patterns of travel need which arise from the necessity to combine paid work, shopping, picking the children up from school and so on. The question of the convenience of public transport is of special signifi-cance to women; women are less likely than men to be car drivers (though less so than previously) and far less likely than men to have primary use of a family car. One can see the effects of this on the gender-specific character of labour market areas.

2.11   Of course, one would not explain women's position in the labour market as a result primarily of such land use patterns and transport structures. Clearly this is a result of gender relations more generally which prescribe certain roles to men, and others to women (see below Section 4.xi), including sex-typing of occupations and other gender divisions of labour in the labour market.

2(iii) The role of infrastructure investment (including resource development) in employment change; the role of landscape and environment in new industrial and service investment

2.12   Recent research reveals that there are a number of important ways in which location, context, environ-ment and built form can influence the economic, especially employment, prospects of areas. One way is through the attractiveness of the rural scenery and the historic nature of the towns. This not only affects tourism, it shapes the pattern of investment in those kinds of activities which need to recruit highly qualified manpower. Another way is through the general eco-nomic effects of urban size. In the past the emphasis was on the positive effects of 'external economies', and this theme is still represented in studies of the agglomeration economies affecting high technology industry, but most of the literature now stresses the disadvantages of urban size. Employment growth can also occur when a major infrastructure investment takes place. A sub-theme of this literature enquires into the employment effects of transport infrastructure investment, such as the road programme, rail invest-ment and disinvestment and airport expansion.

2.13   A special instance of this is the debate about the economic and employment generating effects of the building of the Channel Tunnel (**Vickerman** 1987). Vickerman's sober analysis begins by distinguishing between the short-run effects, which are likely to be greatest in Kent (construction activity) and in the East and West Midlands, and the long-run effects. These long-run effects are extremely difficult to estimate. He inclines to the view that the Channel Tunnel will not affect British regions differentially as far as production is concerned, because there is no region-specific low accessibility problem that the building of the Tunnel will solve. And he adds that poor accessibility as a whole is not the reason for the poor performance of British industry. He then discusses the impact of the Tunnel on the level of demand for the South East region's goods and services using the notion of market potential. This measures the aggregate accessibility of one region to all of the others — in this case the regions of the European Community. Even if the Tunnel were to be 100% efficient (i.e. equivalent to land distance as a friction effect), it would only increase the South East's potential by 5%. He then shows that Kent has an employment structure which reflects the fact that it is on the wrong side of the south/south divide, with low presence of high growth sectors in both manufacturing and the services. He believes that some improvement in this respect might follow from the building of the Tunnel, but suggests that the effects may be less in manufacturing, where transport costs are a very small proportion of value added, than in the distribution sector. He estimates that the cost-reduction effects of the Tunnel will have only a marginal effect on the level of cross-Channel traffic, and admits that there is much uncertainty about the outcome of the competition between the Tunnel and the ferry operators. He does, however, expect the excursion traffic to increase, and the rail link between London and Paris will be fast enough at three and a quarter hours to capture some air traffic. Finally, he argues that transport barriers have remained as a useful non-tariff barrier within the Community; but he adds that it could be that the cost penalty imposed by the Channel is a greater barrier to imports than to exports!

2(iv) Site constraint effects on the urban/rural shift in manufacturing employment; the land factor in industrial location

2.14   Once built form (houses, factories, roads, air-ports, offices, shopping centres) exists, it has the potential to shape the character and pace of subse-quent economic and social development. In general, as time passes the built form which was suited to an earlier period becomes more and more out of line with present needs, and acts as a constraint upon progress and efficiency. This line of argument has had a long history in the literature of urban change. But in the late 1970s and early 1980s it appeared in a much more empirical form in the work of Fothergill et al on the urban to rural shift in manufacturing employment. **Fothergill and Gudgin** (1983), for example, begin their study of urban and regional employment with the well tried and trusted method of shift-share analysis. It soon became clear, however, that this traditional method of economic analysis was no longer performing in the manner expected of it. In the early post-war period the 'structural' component, accounted for by national trends in employment by sector, was paramount; this meant that if one knew the employment mix of a particular place and the national rates of employment change by sector, one could predict fairly accurately what the employment change in that place would be. The 'differential' component, which represented the deviation of the actual from the expected, was small by comparison. But by the late 1960s and early 1970s this was no longer the case. The differential component had become far more important than the structural component, and what is more, the deviations seemed to be all in one direction only — the more urban and industrial the region, the greater the actual employment fell short of the expected; the more the region was characterised by freestanding cities and small and medium-sized towns, the greater the actual employment exceeded the expected.

2.15 Fothergill and Gudgin were particularly interested in manufacturing employment. They showed that there was a marked urban-rural shift in manufacturing employment during the 1960s and early 1970s, and they investigated the alternative explanations for this shift. They convincingly demonstrated that industrial structure was not the cause since the advantageous structures were to be found in the regions which were losing manufacturing jobs most rapidly, notably South East England. They then show that government regional policy, though significant for part of the time, cannot be regarded as the principal factor either. Many urban areas in receipt of regional assistance lost manufacturing jobs, whereas many rural areas, not in receipt of such assistance, gained. The size structure of firms was important because manufacturing employment growth was positively associated with areas characterised by small firms; areas dominated by large firms seemed to deter employment growth. Finally, they concluded that the key factor was urban structure, that is, the size of the city; large ones lost manufacturing jobs, small ones gained. This was interpreted to mean that the site constraints experienced by firms operating in the existing industrial cities limited their opportunities to reorganise their production to increase productivity and thus stay competitive, or to expand production to maintain or increase their market share, whereas in small and medium-sized towns no such site constraints existed.

2.16 However, changes in industrial location occur for a number of good reasons other than floorspace and site development problems in the constrained locations of the conurbations. There is a need to focus attention on labour force issues, for example, and on the wider corporate restructuring and investment patterns of industry (see Chapter 4 below).

Evaluation

2.16 Our main findings in relation to the literature reviewed in this chapter are as follows:

(i) that it is valid to argue that spatial structures and built forms become increasingly disfunctional with the passing of time, and that patterns of urban change today will partly reflect the attempts by economic actors to avoid the disadvantages of working within these outmoded physical structures. That these structures have different effects for different groups in the population is also to be expected;

(ii) but that there has been a tendency to place too much weight on this line of argument, to the point of excluding almost all other considerations. One would not explain women's position in the labour market as resulting primarily from the present day effects of past land use patterns and transportation networks. Similarly, it would be unwise to interpret high unemployment primarily in terms of a maldistributed housing stock, or deindustrialisation in terms of inner city built form obsolescence. In particular, there are many problems with the argument that housing policies exacerbate unemployment. If all housing were offered at market prices or rents in high growth regions, housing costs would be higher than they are at present which would mean higher wages and hence fewer jobs. Thus complicated interdependencies exist. Above all, owner occupiers in declining regions would find it very difficult to move because of the immense differentials in house prices between high growth and low growth regions. There is therefore no certainty that a 'freeing up' of the housing market would reduce unemployment; and

(iii) the policy implication of this judgement is that there are limitations to the possibilities of using housing and infrastructure investments, urban physical regeneration or environmental improvements to effect an increase in urban job prospects and living standards. Clearly, there are other parts to the equation.

CHAPTER 3

The role of housing and built form in shaping social relations

Issues

3.1 This Chapter reviews literature on the ways in which the built environment influences the experiences, behaviours and relationships of individuals and groups. There are two main questions to be confronted:

(i) what effects do the design and physical layout of housing and the built environment have on the behaviour of individuals and on their social relationships? Debates on this issue tend to polarise between two extreme positions: (a) those who say that the building designs of the 'modern movement' in architecture are to blame for the social problems found in many parts of our cities, notably those with large high rise council estates; and (b) those who turn to social structure for an explanation of social problems. Is physical space no more than a backdrop for social processes so that physical space per se has no social effect, or is the organisation of physical space a contingent factor which may in certain circumstances affect the way in which causal mechanisms operate, or, finally, does physical space actually cause or determine social behaviour? and

(ii) what is the social significance of housing, or more specifically, of housing tenure? While housing tenure will obviously reflect social relations (for example, occupation, ethnicity, and stage in the life-cycle), does tenure also 'constitute' or help to produce social relations? Does owner-occupation create economic advantages denied to other tenures? Is owner-occupation associated with specific cultural practices, for instance individualism, privatism and the undermining of collective behaviours? What are the implications of mass owner-occupation for those remaining in other tenures, particularly public sector housing? Is

there a growing marginalisation and stigmatisation of council tenants? Is there a polarisation between home owners and tenants which is leading to the growth of an urban 'underclass'?

3(i) Effects of urban design on human behaviour: the responsibility of council estate layout and built form for crime, vandalism etc

3.2 The debate about the role of space/spatial structure in determining society/social relations, sometimes couched in the language of 'environmental' or 'architectural determinism', has a long history. In the late 19th and early 20th centuries it centred on the role of cities in transforming social relations. Rural areas were regarded as conducive to the establishment of close-knit communities, whereas in the cities, community relationships broke down and most social contacts were between strangers. This resulted from the size of the city and the functional complexity of urban life. The debate continues today with some authors asserting the centrality of time and space in social theory (notably Giddens in his 'Contemporary Critique of Historical Materialism'), while others only ascribe to spatial organisation the power to inhibit or facilitate the development of certain processes in society.

3.3 Recent empirical research relating to this theme focuses on two broad issues: the first concerns the gender significance of urban built form. Specifically it considers women and the man-made environment, and argues that built form both expresses, and serves to reproduce, gender inequality in UK society. The second case concerns housing estate design and urban social problems. For more than half a century much urban and regional research seems to have been dedicated to

15

denying the importance of physical space. Physical space has been largely treated as a passive backdrop against which broad social relationships and processes are played out. More specifically, the relationships between physical space and individual behaviour have been assumed away. Recently, however, these silences and omissions in housing and urban studies have begun to be discussed again; they have been opened up as part of a sustained attack on architects and planners. The argument is that those responsible for organising physical space (in particular for the construction of high rise housing estates and highly segregated residential areas) are systematically denying peoples' needs for everyday association and for the assertion of their identity within society.

3.4   The debate, however, has been opened up in a highly charged way. Much of it focuses on **Alice Coleman's** 'Utopia on Trial' (1985) in which it is suggested that the physical environments built by the 'modern movement' in architecture are largely responsible for a wide range of contemporary problems. Drawing her evidence from over 4,000 blocks of flats, Coleman claims that a number of indicators of social malaise (including children taken into care, vandalism, graffiti, urine and faeces) are correlated with a range of design factors such as the number of dwellings in a block, the height of blocks, the extent to which they are linked to each other, the number of entry points to each development and the number of dwelling units served by each entrance.

3.5   Coleman's work is closely linked to similar recent research on the effects of architectural design on various forms of criminal behaviour. The argument is that certain forms of physical design (including through routes providing easy escape, the lack of semi-public observable space and the proximity of residential areas to other land uses such as industry) are closely associated with burglary, pick-pocketing, assault and rape. And recently this kind of analysis has found its way into official government policy; the current 'Crime. Together we'll crack it!' campaign gives considerable coverage to the role of architectural design. Amongst the measures recommended are individual front gardens to encourage responsibility, windows facing the street to make observation easy, and mixed housing to encourage social integration (see 3.28 for a critique of this position).

3.6   The work of **Hillier and Hanson** (1984) becomes central to this discussion when they begin to explore the social implications of alternative spatial arrangements and to suggest that some kinds of spatial relationship may be facilitating social interaction more than others. They argue that, to an increasing extent, contemporary urban and neighbourhood design militates against human encounters, everyday contact and social interaction. They use their mathematical 'spatial syntax' methods to analyse the spatial organi-

sation of a number of pre-industrial and early industrial towns, and they conclude that many of these old urban areas were so designed that people could have a strong sense of their urban area as a whole. This is because streets and public squares were not designed as relatively isolated social units, separated from the rest of the town's physical and social structure. The space syntax measures of the connectivity of physical spaces shows that the degree of connectedness within urban spatial structures is much less in contemporary town planning. The principles of the modern movement combined with the spatial determinism which led architects and planners to think that they could literally construct separate communities through, for example, the design of separated housing estates, militates not only against the intelligibility of our cities to individual residents but against what Hillier and Hanson call 'virtual community' or 'co-presence and encounter'. This is interaction in the form of awareness of, and interaction with, other people, whether these people are familiar or strangers.

3.7   So what are we to conclude as regards the implications for urban and housing research of this recent literature on the role of physical space in human behaviour and social life? Housing and urban studies currently contain a number of different assumptions about the role of physical space:

(a) the first (and arguably the most common) assumption is that physical space has itself no social effects. Such a view suggests that social processes and relationships simply impose themselves on physical structures. However, this rejection of the role of physical space seems premature. With many aspects of individual behaviour not yet understood, and given that alternative spatial forms do seem to have effects on levels and forms of day-to-day interaction, such a 'passive' view of space seems unjustified;

(b) a second view would be to see physical space as a 'contingent' factor. Social relationships (such as those of class, gender or race) are here seen as the prime active causal mechanisms underlying social change. The precise form they take, however, might be affected by physical space. A block of flats, for example, may, as the modernist architects intended, be a setting for a thriving and supportive community life. It may also be, as in the case of the Broadwater Farm, the setting for a full-scale riot against the police. Physical space is seen as being contingent; it affects the form of important underlying relations (those between classes, or between people and police) but is not in itself a major mechanism affecting social change.

3(ii)   Housing influences on social relations; age and ethnicity

3.8   In this section and in the two sections to come, we review the literature on the significance of housing for social change in urban areas in contemporary Britain. The core element in this theme is the social impact of owner occupation and of its recent growth in relation to other tenure groups. But in this first section we review studies of the significance of housing for different social groups such as ethnic minorities, young people, women and the elderly.

3.9 People's housing situation is obviously influenced and shaped by their social situation. Where they live, the quality of their accommodation and whether they buy or rent are all dependent to some degree on social factors such as the jobs they do, their age and stage in the life cycle, their ethnicity, and so on. However, housing does not simply reflect social relations. It also helps to constitute them. This is true both as regards the physical form and structure of housing, and as regards the way it is organised socially. Physical form enables some kinds of social activity while constraining others. The design and size of accommodation may, for example, make it difficult to establish privacy or to maintain security. Similarly, the form of the relationship between individuals in households and the housing they occupy also affects how people live. A household which owns its home, for example, may find that it can do things which are prohibited to people who rent.

3.10 Contemporary research on the significance of housing tenure for social relations originated in the study of housing and race in Birmingham by Rex and Moore (in Race, Community and Conflict). To help them to understand the competitive struggle for housing which seemed to be going on in the city, Rex and Moore developed the concept of 'housing classes'. They identified six such classes (although the list was later extended), and these were based on divisions between and within tenure groups. Thus, the most privileged housing classes were the outright owners and mortgage purchasers of suburban houses; they were followed by tenants of purpose-built council housing and tenants in poorer quality local authority stock; and at the bottom were landlords of inner city sub-divided properties and their tenants. These six groups struggled against each other to secure access to scarce and desirable housing in either the private or public sectors.

3.11 While many later authors have contested the theoretical basis for Rex and Moore's work (see next section), the research interest in housing and social inequality, and housing and race, has continued. In particular, as ethnic minority households have increasingly entered public sector housing, there has been a concern to discover how the allocation mechanisms operate to affect their welfare. This research on housing and race shows that despite legislation against racial discrimination and the fact that the majority of black people are now long standing residents of the UK

(40% of them born in Britain), racial disadvantage in housing persists. Black people live in older and less desirable housing in both the public and the private sectors of the housing market, as tenants they pay higher rent, and as potential purchasers of housing they face more difficulty in obtaining mortgage finance, and tend to finish up owning property in inner urban areas which are costly to maintain and slow to increase in value. A major theme of recent writing has been that, as with gender inequality, racial inequality is not just reflected in the housing situations that black people find themselves in, it is also actively sustained and reproduced by the housing system.

3.12 Closely related to the housing and race theme, due to the spatial segregation of ethnic minorities, is that of low-income owner occupation in the inner city. A key piece of research in this respect is the study by **Karn, Kemeny and Williams** (1985). They show from their surveys in Birmingham and Liverpool that, although home-ownership in the inner city is increasing rapidly, it is not providing the inhabitants there with the benefits which it endows those who are owner occupiers elsewhere in the urban system. In particular, many Asian buyers were paying higher than market rates of interest to purchase housing which was in very poor condition, and which was falling in price, in relation to other housing in the region, partly because the building societies regarded it as a bad risk (thus ensuring that it was so!). The state of disrepair of the housing was given particular emphasis in this study; and one remarkable finding was that the estimated mean cost of improvement to a 30-year life was more than the mean price paid for the houses.

3.13 Many of these problems of inner city home ownership are faced by other disadvantaged groups in our society such as single parent households (very predominantly female headed), and, more generally, by young people attempting to enter home ownership. In this context, with house purchase so often depending upon two incomes, it is particularly interesting to enquire into the relationships between housing tenure and family formation. At the same time a lively literature is developing on the housing situations of the elderly, and on the single homeless.

3(iii) **Housing influences on social relations; the social significance of owner occupation**

3.14 Out of the earlier debate on housing and race came a new concern to analyse the sociological significance of tenurial divisions in British society. In particular, as home ownership has increased from 10% of households in 1914 to nearly two-thirds today, so research has focussed on what effect, if any, the spread of owner occupation is having on social relations in this country.

3.15 Initially, debate on this issue polarised. For the Marxists social class was what mattered, and housing tenure was at most an ideological phenomenon serving to confuse lines of class cleavage. Against them stood those such as **Peter Saunders** who argued that ownership of domestic property generated a new and real social cleavage, such that owner-occupiers constituted a distinct social stratum with their own interests which often brought them into conflict with tenants (Saunders 1984).

3.16 For Saunders the debate basically revolves around three core questions. First, does owner-occupation create economic advantages which are denied to tenants? Second, is it associated with particular cultural changes such a growth in privatised lifestyles or increased individualism? And third, does it encourage shifts in political alignment by influencing working class voters to desert the Labour Party and to support market alternatives to welfare? Much of the literature on the third of these questions is considered elsewhere in this report (Section 7.6). He argues that home ownership is not a homogeneous category (in which case the significance of tenure should not be generalised), nevertheless it does produce substantial economic advantages for many owners, and it does allow many people to give expression to deeply held values of independence and autonomy. To this extent, tenure divisions do generate new lines of inequality and cleavage in our society, and the division between the relatively privileged stratum of home owners and the increasingly marginalised stratum of poor council tenants seems to be widening.

3.17 According to Ray Pahl in 'Whose City' a family may gain more from the housing market in a few years than would be possible in savings from a lifetime of earnings. If this is the case, then it would indicate that the growth of home ownership since the war has been crucial in redistributing wealth and reshaping inequalities. In 1960, 20% of personal wealth was represented by owner-occupied housing; today it is over 50%. The Diamond Commission on the Distribution of Income and Wealth showed that, if housing is included in the calculations, the wealth gap between the rich and the average household has narrowed considerably. Of course, this would also suggest that the gap between home owners and tenants has been widening, for capital gains on housing are clearly not available to tenants. The growth of owner-occupation, therefore, may be said to have enhanced the wealth of nearly two-thirds of the population while at the same time widening the gap between them and the poorest one third. This then gives rise to arguments about tenure polarisation and the marginalisation of a new underclass.

3.18 It has been argued that none of this really constitutes capital gains in any meaningful sense since the capital cannot be realised for spending on other purposes. Similarly, calculations of capital gains are often crude, neglecting factors like the costs of maintenance, repair and improvement. Some studies even forget to allow for inflation. These arguments shift the focus of attention to the question of whether and how owner-occupiers cash in on their assets. Empirical research on this question is still poorly developed, but there appear to be three main ways in which housing capital can be realised: through inheritance; through equity leakage; and through trading down or other strategies available to older owner-occupiers. For Saunders the question of inheritance is crucial. For the first time a majority of people in Britain can now expect to inherit what may be substantial sums on the death of their parents. This will have various economic implications and it may well encourage the children of home owners to reduce insurance and other provisions towards their old age. Its implications for social structure are also profound, for the division between owners and tenants may become most marked in the next generation. Those not owning their dwellings in the year 2000 are likely to be a small, poor and politically ineffective minority.

3.19 Equity leakage occurs when home owners remortgage (often when they move) and use part of the advance for expenditure on items other than housing. The most extreme recent estimate suggests that as much as 50% of mortgage lending is now leaking into other forms of consumer expenditure. This is almost certainly an overestimate; but it is becoming increasingly possible to borrow for consumer spending against the value of owner occupied housing thereby unlocking some of the equity. The third strategy for realising capital gains is through trading down, either by moving to a smaller house (which becomes possible when children have left home) or by moving to a cheaper area (for example, moving on retirement to a seaside town or rural area). Again, we know remarkably little about this. Alternatively, it may now be possible for older owner-occupiers to stay put and raise capital through various financial schemes. This is then likely to encourage the increased use of private services to the elderly, thereby carrying the division between owners and tenants into provision for old age.

3.20 Capital gains, then, are often realisable. It is also patently the case that not all owner-occupiers make similar gains, and, for some, home ownership may prove a burden rather than an asset. There are major economic differences, for example, between people like high level managers, who often receive considerable assistance from their companies (for example, subsidised mortgages, removal costs, etc), and those at the margins of home ownership. There also appear to be important regional differences in rates of capital gain available to home owners, although in areas of lower house prices, reduced capital gains are to some extent compensated by lower current housing costs. There may even be differences between different housing sub-markets within towns.

3.21 Not only are the gains uneven, but the expansion of home ownership (for example, through council house sales) appears to have brought some casualties with it, especially since it coincided with the recession of the early 1980s. Mortgage arrears of between six and twelve months have risen from 8400 in 1979 to over 50,000 in 1987, and repossessions by lending institutions have increased from under 3000 to over 21,000 in the same period (Social Trends 1988, Table 8.17). Mortgage arrears and foreclosures have received considerable research attention.

3.22 The idea that home ownership encourages individualism and undermines collectivistic values and practices has a long history. Various government papers and building society reports through this century have supported the spread of owner occupation as a means of giving working people a stake in private property. This idea of home ownership as a 'bulwark against bolshevism' has been used by critics to argue that home ownership has been encouraged as a way of fostering individualism and eroding collectivism in the working class. But what evidence is there that home ownership actually has this effect?

3.23 Our thinking here seems to rely heavily on sociological work done in the 1950s and 1960s — in particular, on community studies which purported to show that the cosiness of traditional working class communities was broken up by rising affluence and the move to suburbia. Suburban home ownership is generally associated with middle class values and family-centred and inward-looking ways of life. Saunders would argue, however, that there are grounds for doubting this stereotype of the privatised home owner. Recent studies have claimed that privatism is not more pronounced now than in the past, and that there is nothing inherent in the fact of owning a house which generates individualistic values and life styles. There is in any case no reason to assume that privatised individualism is necessarily incompatible with collective organisation (a point which the famous 'affluent worker' research of the 1960s also emphasised). Indeed, it can be argued that the economic and psychological security which home ownership brings for many people is a condition of their willingness to engage in collective activity. The issue of autonomy appears crucial in all of this. Home ownership, it seems, is virtually a precondition for self-help and self-reliance in other areas of life, and this is one reason why home ownership has been so attractive to many groups. Property is experienced by many people as a basis of individual liberty, autonomy, identity and security and one reason for the overwhelming preference for home ownership, even among council tenants,

is the desire to secure a private and personal realm relatively free from outside intrusion.

3(iv) Housing influences on social relations; housing and social polarisation, private and public rented housing

3.24 With the growth of owner-occupation and the reduction of the public housing stock through sales, some commentators have argued that council housing is becoming a marginalised and stigmatised sector. These arguments to some extent run parallel with concern about the growth of a new 'underclass' in Britain (see Section 7.3), for the distinction between such a group and the 'middle class' does seem to correspond to some extent with that between public sector tenants and owner-occupiers. However, it is obvious that many council tenants do not belong to such a group. Dahrendorf (in his New Statesman article of 12/6/87) estimates the size of the underclass at around five percent of the population (which compares with one quarter of the population in public rented housing), and many of these will be found living in private rented accommodation in inner city areas rather than on suburban council estates.

3.25 Work by **Forrest and Murie** at the School of Advanced Urban Studies (SAUS) at Bristol University has shown how council tenants are becoming marginalised as younger and relatively more affluent tenants take advantage of the discounts offered to buy their homes (Forrest and Murie 1988). The result is that council tenancy is increasingly coming to be more associated with indicators of deprivation — poverty, unemployment, broken families, ethnic minorities, the elderly. As Forrest and Murie put it in an earlier paper, 'whilst the mass of those in employment are being drawn into privatised forms of commodity consumption those on the margin experience a reduction in the quality and level of state-provided services and benefits'.

3.26 This process of polarisation also has a significant regional dimension. Various studies have shown that council housing has been sold mainly in areas which already have relatively high owner-occupancy rates. Sales are mostly of good quality houses in suburban areas, not flats in inner city areas. Sales are also highest in the South of England, partly because property here is more expensive (hence discounts are more valuable), partly because wages are higher and unemployment is lower, and partly because of differences in cultural factors.

3.27 Two qualifications, however, need to be made. The first is that polarisation can occur within the owner-occupation sector, as well as between owner-occupation and renting, as evidenced by the segmentation of the private housing market and mortgage payment default. The second arises from studies of the private rented sector which connects with owner-occupation not only through the process of tenure switching, but also through its use as a first entry into the housing market by young people who eventually become middle class homeowners.

Evaluation

3.28 Our main findings in relation to the literature revised in this chapter are:

(i) that owner-occupation is not a homogeneous category; but

(ii) that it does confer widespread substantial economic advantages on many people, and it does allow the expression of autonomy and independence (though usually at the price of debt encumbrance). Therefore tenure can create social cleavages. The evidence seems to suggest that the cleavage between home owners and renters is widening. The policy implications of this are that those areas, such as parts of the inner cities, which still have high proportions of people living in rented accommodation are likely to contain an increasing proportion of the poorest and most dependent people in the country; and

(iii) that as far as the effect of built form on social relations is concerned, some of the claims emanating from recent research, notably by Alice Coleman, are not sustainable in the face of the criticisms that this research has provoked. Coleman overestimates the significance of design at the expense of social relations and social processes. She ignores the condition (for example, the poverty) of the tenants. An obvious rejoinder to 'Utopia on Trial' is to ask why high rise flats in Bayswater and the Barbican are not slums. According to this view, social and political structures rather than individuals and physical space lie at the root of the problem. Yet these criticisms of Coleman leave some important questions unanswered and her ideas have gained popularity with many on the political left and right.

CHAPTER 4

Urban employment change in the UK: patterns and processes

4.1 The literature on employment change in UK cities is very extensive. It is difficult to envisage anything more central to urban change in the UK than the decline in employment opportunities in most major cities during the 1970s — a decline which reached crisis proportions in the first years of the 1980s. It left many young people unable to enter employment, forced many older people out of it, and modified the expectations of those who remained in it. Similarly, what could be more important to an understanding of the growth of very many small and medium-sized towns in the 1970s, and of London and the South of England more generally in the 1980s, than the location of new jobs in those areas? Much of this growth was in sectors which normally employed women, and the part-time, sometimes temporary nature of the new jobs tended to reinforce female take-up. However, substantial growth also took place in the better paid and relatively secure parts of the service class.

Issues

4.2 Many issues have been raised in this very extensive literature. They include:

(a) General questions, such as:

(i) in what ways has employment changed since 1970?

(ii) where have these changes taken place?

(iii) how did these changes come about?

(iv) why did these changes occur?

(v) and how did these changes affect the relationships between work and employment?

And (b) more specific questions such as:

(i) why was there such a precipitous decline in manufacturing employment, and why was that decline so heavily concentrated in the largest cities, and especially in the inner parts of those cities? Did larger firms shed proportionately more jobs than smaller ones? What determined which establishments survived and which closed? What kinds of workers lost their jobs? Which branches of manufacturing were most affected by job loss? Why did some cities fare better than others? How is the structure of industry changing as employers adapt to changing market conditions?

(ii) why were there major differences between men and women in their employment trends and in their spatial patterns of job loss and gain? In what sense, if any, can one talk of a 'feminisation' of the workforce? To what extent is the increased participation of women due to the differing rates of growth and decline of sectors with differing propensities to employ women? To what extent, if any, has there been a direct substitution of women for men in particular jobs? Is gender segregation in employment changing? If so, in what ways, where and why?

(iii) how does one account for the growth of the producer services, and to what extent was this growth responsible for the turnround in the London economy experienced in the 1980s? More generally, why was it that service employment growth compensated manufacturing employment decline in some cities and not in others? Did the contribution of the public sector services to employment change differ from that of the private sector, and if so, where and why? And

(iv) is there substance to the notion of 'flexible specialisation', and if so, does it have a geography?

What are the locational requirements and implications of new and restructured technical and employment relations? What is the nature of high-tech employment? Where is it located and why?

Contributions

4.3   With such a large and varied, yet interconnected, literature it is inevitable that a classification of the contributions will be somewhat arbitrary. No simple relationship between the categories used in reviewing the literature and the issues raised above is to be expected. The categories used are:

(i) general studies of economic restructuring and labour market change; work in the formal, informal and domestic economies;

(ii) urban regional economic change; regional economics;

(iii) urban and regional employment change; emerging spatial divisions of labour;

(iv) studies of urban and regional changes in unemployment;

(v) the anatomy of manufacturing job loss; the urban/rural shift in manufacturing employment;

(vi) the location of high technology industry; the U.K. sunbelt;

(vii) urban and regional employment change in the services;

(viii) new service employment; the changing geography of producer services;

(ix) flexibility; new forms of work organisation; self-employment;

(x) youth labour markets; training and recruitment; early retirement;

(xi) jobs and gender; 'feminisation' in local labour markets; and

(xii) race and employment; immigrant workers.

4(i) General studies of economic restructuring and labour market change; work in the formal, informal and domestic economies

4.4   Two main themes dominate the general literature on changes in work and employment in the recent period. The first is an insistence that local change can only be understood properly when it is placed in the context of change in the national and international economies. Thus the increase in local unemployment which is consequent upon the deindustrialisation of many British cities is related to the poor competitiveness of British manufacturing in the face of fierce competition from producers in the Far East and elsewhere. The second theme is an awareness of the multi-faceted nature of work, and of the perviousness of the boundaries between employment, informal labour, domestic labour and leisure.

4.5   This second theme is neatly developed by **Ray Pahl** in the Epilogue to his edited collection of essays 'On Work'. Pahl shows by means of the image of a woman standing at an ironing board, that one cannot know whether she is engaged in wage labour, informal work, domestic labour or pleasure without knowing the social relations of the ironing activity. As a domestic outworker she might be employed full-time, part-time or casually, and be legally-registered or hired informally. She might be self-employed producing garments for sale, perhaps employing others in the process, in which case she is engaged in petty commodity production, or is a small-scale capitalist. Alternatively, she is not earning income from the activity but is carrying out a domestic task. Pahl asks, is she ironing a garment to give pleasure to someone she loves, or fulfilling a much resented domestic duty for a domineering husband or demanding mother-in-law? Even if she is ironing her own clothes one needs to know if they are to be worn 'at work' or at some social occasion. Finally, it is possible that she is neither working for money nor servicing the household but is doing a favour for someone, perhaps in the hope that the favour will be reciprocated. We may have reservations about ironing for pleasure and the sex-stereotyping in Pahl's example, but he uses it to make a number of important points. He insists, for example, that it would be wrong to say that the woman was not working when she was not engaging in wage labour. So work is not to be equated with paid employment. Also her orientation to the task was important because it substantially affected the form of work in which she was engaged, whether or not, for example, it was exploitative in nature.

4.6   These arguments have a particular significance to the literature on changes in work and employment in British cities, because hardly any of this research is concerned with work outside employment, and few of the studies inquire into the attitudes of those engaged in the work, or into the social contexts of their activities.

4(ii) Urban and regional economic change; regional economic studies

4.7   Central to an understanding of all the other aspects of urban change in the UK is knowledge of how and why the economies of urban areas have changed over the recent period. At the forefront of research on this topic has been the ESRC's Inner Cities Research Programme (ICRP). The ICRP grew out of the Inner Cities in Context (ICIC) research which was carried out during the period 1977–80. Indeed, its form follows, in almost every detail, that proposed by Peter Hall and Derek Diamond in their final chapter of the ICIC report. The ICRP began in 1982 and was generously funded by the ESRC, topped up later by the DoE. The productivity of the group under the Directorship of **Victor Hausner** has been very considerable; eight books have already appeared and two more are on the way. Five of the eight volumes are case studies of urban change (London, Bristol, Birmingham, Newcastle and Glasgow), and a further volume summarises the findings from these case studies. The two other books represent 'cross-cutting' studies which analyse aspects of urban and inner city economic change at the level of Britain as a whole. The emphasis throughout is on economic restructuring and its impact on disadvantaged groups, on the workings of the urban land and labour markets, and on central and local government economic policies.

4.8   A good example of one of the 'cross-cutting' studies is the overview chapter in the Hausner edited volume 1 of 'Critical Issues in Urban Economic Development' by Begg, Moore and Rhodes entitled 'Economic and Social Change in Urban Britain and the Inner Cities'. This statistical overview covers the 1951–81 period; it focuses upon changes in the population of working age, changes in employment and unemployment, and changes in commuting and in employment by sector. Its areal units are the inner and outer areas of the six largest conurbations, the seventeen largest remaining cities, and the rest of Britain. The statistics produced are very striking. They show how, as employment growth in Britain in the 1950s turned to employment decline in the 1970s, it was the precipitous decline in manufacturing employment, particularly in the largest cities, and most particularly in the inner areas of these cities, which led the way. Two sets of calculations comprise the more analytical sections of the paper. The first results in labour market balance sheets for the case study cities, or, to be more exact, for the pre-1974 administrative areas of those cities; the second results in measures of the statistical association between employment decline and a set of deprivation indices. This shows that the job losses were most likely to occur in areas with high and growing proportions of: (i) unemployed people; (ii) single-parent families; and (iii) households without a car. These kinds of result tell us little, if anything, about the processes of urban change, but they suggest that people who live in areas where problems were already serious, were likely to see their situations made worse by further job losses.

4.9   In the volume which summarises the material contained in the five case studies, Hausner points to the main explanations for this employment decline in the major cities, and especially in their inner areas. Firstly, he stresses the importance of the inherited industrial structure, and the effects of economic restructuring as firms closed plants or shed labour to remain competitive in the face of heightened international competition. A heavy dependence upon manufacturing industry increased the likelihood of job loss, but the sectoral structure of the manufacturing mattered less than its location, with job losses concentrated in the largest cities and in the inner parts of those cities. Indigenous firms in old industrial cities showed poor economic performance, with low productivity due to out-moded technology and poor industrial relations. The external control of the many other firms led to them being vulnerable to contraction and closure, and meant that there was little demand for producer services due to the lack of senior management activities. Futhermore, the urban economies which were dominated by manufacturing industry were also seemingly unsuited to the growth of new firms, due to skill inflexibilities, low mobility, low levels of entrepreneurial activity and a lack of innovation. However, it was not the contribution of new jobs in small firms which was the main factor which differentiated the employment changes experienced by the five case study cities; it was instead the slower decline of Bristol's defence-related larger firms, in comparison with the rapid declines of the major manufacturing firms in Glasgow, Newcastle and Birmingham. Bristol also benefited from the decentralisation of office employment from London due to the high costs of land and labour in the capital. London's economic performance was poor in manufacturing but it gained from its role as the national centre of administration, management, finance, culture and tourism.

4(iii)   **Urban and regional employment change; emerging spatial divisions of labour**

4.10   A major development of the last ten to fifteen years has been the use of concepts of political economy, some of it Marxist inspired, to achieve a better understanding of these processes of urban and regional economic change. One field in which this is most noticeable is in the study of 'external control'. This refers to the way in which urban and regional economies have increasingly become dependent upon the operations of firms and organisations whose head offices, research and development activities and, above all, ownership, are external to the region in question. Much of this important work is conformable with Doreen Massey's argument, first developed in the late 1970s (see in particular her paper published in Regional Studies in 1979 entitled 'In what sense a regional problem?'), that regional economic problems can persist, even intensify, during a period in which standard indicators of economic performance (notably unemployment rates and net migration gains and losses) seem to be pointing towards regional economic convergence. The reason for this is that the number of jobs and people in the regions is no guide to the quality of those jobs or of the lives of the people doing them. With a spatial separation of conception and control from routine production, and a concentration of the former in the southern regions of England, especially in London, and of the latter in the North and West of the UK, a 'new spatial division of labour' comes into being and with it comes a new geography of wealth and power which is not reflected in the unemployment and net migration statistics.

4.11 Accompanying these conceptual developments there was a sudden increase in the volume of empirical research on urban and regional employment change. The main patterns of employment change as described in this literature are as follows:

(i) a rapid decline in manufacturing employment from the late 1960s until the late 1980s at the national level, made up of massive declines in the major cities (including London), slower declines in many medium-sized towns, and some growth in many small towns and rural areas;

(ii) differential job loss between industrial sectors. But the declines were by no means confined to the heavy industries such as coal-mining, steel manufacture and shipbuilding, nor to the traditional 'problem' regions dominated by these industries. Thus many of the cities associated with the consumer goods boom of the 1950s and 1960s, such as London, Birmingham and Coventry, also experienced rapid job losses in manufacturing industry;

(iii) a growth in female employment, much of it part-time. This was partly associated with branch plant investment in the 1960s and early 1970s in industrial regions such as South Wales and the North East, and in small and medium-sized towns in rural areas, but it was mostly, and more generally, associated with an increase in service employment;

(iv) service employment growth was not enough at the national level to offset the massive declines during the 1970s and early 1980s in manufacturing industry, but it occurred at every level of the urban system and contributed greatly to the employment growth of free standing cities, small and medium-sized towns in rural areas and towns within metropolitan city regions;

(v) within the services, there were pronounced differences between sectors, with employment growth in the education and health services figuring prominently in the late 1960s and early 1970s, to be replaced by banking and business services in the late 1970s and early 1980s. This latter growth was not confined to South East England, but it was there that it made a substantial contribution to total employment change; and

(vi) finally, there were important shifts in employment by size of establishment. Employment in large establishments declined sharply after 1970, while employment in small establishments increased as did self-employment. Once again this was a spatially selective process; labour markets dominated by large employers tended to be in the Midlands and North, and this is where the job losses were most severe.

4.12 Despite the number of empirical studies of employment change, with one or two very important exceptions the analysis of local and regional labour markets was, until recently, rather poorly developed in the UK. During the late 1970s and 1980s this has changed as economists and others have tried to explain how local labour markets have been affected by recession and by the changes which have been provoked by recession. One early debate centred on the role of employment 'mismatch' in explaining inner city unemployment. The DoE inner city studies had tended to draw upon the 'Kain Thesis' that inner city workers were disadvantaged by the suburbanisation of employment towards areas from which they were excluded by the high cost of housing. This was questioned by those who pointed out that demand deficiency always hits the unskilled workers hardest, and that it is in the inner city that such workers are to be found in the greatest concentration. Since then much of the emphasis has been upon the economic modelling of the relations between employment change and unemployment, on the workings of inner city labour markets, on the relationship between earnings and unemployment, and on the role of labour mobility in effecting changes in employment and unemployment.

4.13 While the dominant element in studies of employment change in UK cities and regions has inevitably been the massive loss of jobs in many major cities, there is a growing body of literature which refers to the patterns of job creation, notably to the growth of jobs in high technology industries and producer services in the so called British 'sunbelt', the area around and to the west of London, stretching from Cambridge, through Oxford, to Bristol and Southampton (see Section 4.6 below).

4(iv) Studies of urban and regional changes in unemployment

4.14 Many would argue that the single most significant fact about urban change in the UK in the recent period has been the dramatic increase in urban unemployment. Compared with the 1960s, the early-mid 1970s saw a marked worsening of the employment situation in every major city. But this was as nothing compared with the changes in the 1979–83 period. Many older men and women lost their jobs and faced the prospect that they would never work again; very many young people had practically no chance of entering the labour market in the foreseeable future. Unemployment rates reached levels not seen since the 1930s, and in many parts of the large industrial cities of northern and western Britain more than half of the working age adults were out of work. One of the main features of the pattern of unemployment was that it was on the increase in all parts of the country — in most of the south as well as in the north, in rural areas as well as in the cities, in the suburbs as well as in the inner city. But equally important was the concentration of the highest rates of increase in the industrial north and west of Britain, in Northern Ireland and, above all, in the West Midlands. The lowest rates of increase were in certain parts of the outer South East and in those areas most affected by the oil developments in northern and northeastern Scotland. Unemployment nationally has declined somewhat since the peak level in 1985, but it still affects between two and three million people in the UK; this is a level which until recently would have been regarded as politically unsustainable.

4.15   Much research effort has been spent on describing and statistically analysing the spatial patterns of unemployment. **Ann Green** (1986) has focussed attention on the long term unemployed; these she shows to be concentrated in the north and west rather than in the south and east, in the major conurbations rather than in the rural areas, and in those cities which are based on manufacturing employment rather than on the services.

4.16   Another important contributor to these debates about urban unemployment, local labour market process and migration has been **Ian Gordon**. In a recent paper (1987) he argues that there is an interdependence between urban and regional demand-deficient unemployment and the attractiveness of workers to employers in an inter-regional, that is, open, employment system. Workers in demand-deficient areas absorb into their work histories those attributes which make them less likely to become employed there or elsewhere.

4(v)   The anatomy of manufacturing job loss; the urban/rural shift in manufacturing employment

4.17   Most studies of the patterns of employment change in urban areas focus on manufacturing job loss. This is in line with the idea that almost all manufacturing employment is 'basic' (in the sense that its products are sold outside the locality of production and are therefore income earners for that locality), while most service employment is 'non-basic' (but see below for a discussion of producer services). Studies of manufacturing job loss tend to fall into two groups depending on the spatial scale of primary interest, that

is, either the urban/rural or the north/south. They also tend to differ from one another in their methods of analysis; some adopt a 'location factors' approach, while others interpret the pattern of job loss in terms of a broader political economy approach.

4.18   A good example of research which adopts the location factors approach to the urban/rural shift in manufacturing employment is the work of **David Keeble** (1980). In his earlier research Keeble had placed considerable emphasis on the role of government regional policy in the pattern of manufacturing employment change (see Section 9.2 for a fuller treatment of this issue). By the late 1970s, however, it was becoming clear that the urban/rural differences were far more significant than the assisted/non-assisted area differences and that much of the new investment in assisted areas would probably have taken place in the absence of policy incentives. One response to this was to emphasise the effect of an outmoded physical fabric in the larger cities on the decentralisation of manufacturing investment (see discussion of the work of Fothergill et al in Chapter 2). Keeble accepts this line of argument to a large extent, but, drawing in part upon the results of questionnaire surveys, he also stresses the importance of selective migration from the larger cities, especially London, and the role of environmental factors in attracting these highly qualified migrants, and the small firm investments with which they are associated, to small and medium-sized towns in rural regions such as East Anglia, the East Midlands and the South West. In both his earlier work and his 1980 paper, Keeble makes manufacturing employment change the dependent variable in regression analyses. The location factors then become the independent variables in the regressions equation. In his earlier work (1976) the statistically significant location factors for the 1966–71 period were the size of the manufacturing sector (as an index of agglomeration diseconomies), residential space preferences and assisted area status; in his 1980 paper 'rurality' and female activity rates came to the fore.

4.19   To explain these changes in manufacturing many came to use the concept of 'deindustrialisation'. The difference between this approach and the location factors approach is that much more attention was paid to what was happening to industry itself. Several interconnected questions were examined: how is the structure of industry changing as employers adapt to changing market and competitive conditions? What determines which establishments survive and which close? What are the locational requirements and implications of new and restructured technical and employment relations? And what impact do geographical conditions play in shaping competitiveness? Quite clearly, this industrial restructuring approach shares many of the concerns of the location factors approach. Its distinctiveness, however, lies in the fact that it integrates them within a wider theoretical perspective: development is not just quantitative but depends on, and transforms, the social complexion of places. Within this framework, moreover, factors are considered interdependent rather than independent. A firm that adopts new technologies, for example, may seek regional aid to finance the new investment. At the same time, the new methods of production may make the old skills of unionised workers redundant, and new cheaper sources of labour may be sought out, also in the assisted areas.

4.20   When it comes to the description and analysis of industrial change (mostly decline in the recent period), the literature is very well developed. Much of this literature is fairly general and deals with the causes and consequences of industrial decline. But two lines of research deserve special mention. **Lloyd and Dicken's** (1983) paper synthesises much of the work of the Manchester University team on the 'components of change' approach. This involves a kind of accounting procedure in which total manufacturing employment change is disaggregated into: (i) change due to firms setting up in the area; (ii) change due to closures; and (iii) change resulting from in situ growth or decline. Each of these is then further disaggregated to permit a comparison between single plant and multiplant firms and between locally-based, UK and foreign, multiplant firms. This approach affords a better description of the outcomes of the processes of industrial change, but does not, in itself, explain what those processes are.

4.21   Massey and Meegan's book entitled 'The Anatomy of Job Loss' has had a considerable influence on studies of industrial change (**Massey and Meegan** 1982). In particular, they emphasise the importance of the processes of reorganisation of production in the face of heightened domestic and (especially) foreign competition. This reorganisation takes three main forms, each with different implications for urban job loss. The first is intensification; this involves the achievement of increased productivity through altered work methods without major new investment or change in the technology of production. Rationalisation achieves productivity increases and greater profitability through the selective closure of parts of a firms operations; the job losses are sudden and severe. Investment and technical change involves the use of new investment in transforming production methods; it can, under certain circumstances, generate new jobs in new locations.

4(vi) The location of high technology industry; the UK sunbelt

4.22   The emphasis so far has been on manufacturing employment decline, but certain small and medium-sized towns and rural areas have seen their manufac-

turing employments increase. In part this is due to the location of high technology industry and related (eg computer) services. In general, high technology is taken to include primarily electronics, but also sectors such as bio-technology, instrument engineering and aerospace. But not all high technology industry employs high proportions of highly skilled labour. This is particularly the case in peripheral regions such as Central Scotland and South Wales.

4.23   Much of the literature emphasises the concentration of high technology industry, and of the related research and development activities of both public and private sector organisations, in southern England, and in particular in the western crescent around and to the west of London. But the attention on the M4 corridor and Cambridge, as areas of innovative high technology industry, and on Scotland and South Wales as areas of branch plant activity, should not obscure the complexity of local and regional situations, or the significance of London itself (and other home counties) in the spatial distribution of these activities. Furthermore, there are significant traces of 'boosterism' in some of the literature on high-tech industry, which serves to weaken its credibility.

4.24   These, and other criticisms of the literature are developed in **Morgan and Sayers'** recent book (1988). They argue that:

(i) despite the spatial divisions of labour literature (see Section 4.3 above), only a few authors explore Britain's place in the international division of labour in the high technology sectors of the economy. Nor are specific localities studied within the sub-national, as well as the international, division of labour. This has led to a lack of concern about the issue of the external control of the industry, which is at a very high level. This, in turn, has led researchers to overestimate the similarities between UK and US high technology concentrations, and hence the scope for 'cloning' them elsewhere;

(ii) it follows from this, that work on location choice frequently falls back upon pre-Massey types of industrial location theory, with its lists and rankings of location factors such as universities, airports etc.;

(iii) explanations of the growth of the western crescent have depended too heavily upon such things as the biographies of the founders, and have been weakened both by the lack of industry-specific contextual information (for example, on competitive situations) and by the absence of an economic theory of industrial growth; and

(iv) while labour market characteristics of the growth areas have rightly received considerable attention, other aspects such as the location of markets for high technology products also require emphasis.

4.25 Finally, important advances have been made in the study of the significant role played by defence expenditure in the location of high technology industries. Several authors have linked the development of electronics firms in the South East and South West regions to the firms' heavy involvement in defence electronics, and to their need for proximity to government defence research and military establishments.

4(vii) Urban and regional employment change in the service sector

4.26 Given the 'basic' (export) nature of most manufacturing employment in urban labour markets, it is not surprising that so much research effort in the recent period has been spent on describing and accounting for manufacturing job loss. However, because of (i) the spatial standardization of many public sector services, and (ii) the maintenance of incomes in high job loss areas through transfer payments (unemployment benefit, pensions, supplementary benefits), manufacturing job loss has not always had the drastic effects on the local economy that one might expect on the basis of urban economic theory. Service employment has often held up, and sometimes even grown, in cities which have experienced rapid manufacturing job loss. As a result the proportion of the workforce employed in the service sector has almost universally increased. At the same time, there are certain services which are themselves 'basic' in character, in that they are produced not just for the local inhabitants, but for a wider regional, national or even international market (some of these are discussed in the next section). The important fact about these 'basic' services is that they have become far more important in the recent period, and, as a result, many urban economies are now, to a large degree, dependent upon them.

4.27 General studies of service sector employment change in UK cities and regions have increased in number and quality over the last few years. Particularly instrumental in this process has been **Peter Daniels** who was publishing books and articles on the service sector when almost all research interest was centred on manufacturing industry (Daniels 1985). What these studies show is not only the very great concentration of service employment in the South East region, but that also, after a period of general service employment growth across almost all cities and regions in the early-mid 1970s (associated with the expansion of public sector services, notably health and education), there was a subsequent reconcentration of service employment growth (now private sector based and centred on financial services) in the three regions of southern England, so that by the mid 1980s the service gap between north and south had distinctively widened.

4(viii) New service employment; the changing geography of producer services

4.28 As interest in service sector employment change has increased it has become clear that it is within certain branches of the so-called 'producer services', notably banking, insurance, property, legal and business services that most of the employment growth has occurred, and that, because of the high incomes that many of the professional staff in these sectors command, this employment has been very important for the operation of urban and regional economies. The recent rapid growth of these kinds of jobs is due to (i) developments in the national economy away from manufacturing industry and towards financial services, and (ii) the increase in the social division of labour which has meant that specialised firms and agencies are now carrying out tasks previously done within large organisations. There is a massive concentration of producer services in the South East region, notably in London, but also in certain sub-centres within the South East such as Croydon, Brighton, Crawley and Reading. Otherwise producer service employment is largely confined to a small number of large provincial cities, notably Manchester, Leeds, Bristol, Norwich and Edinburgh. Recent growth in producer services employment has been in the City of London, in certain back office locations in southern England and in certain provincial cities, but not in major cities such as Liverpool. The growth in London has been considerably enhanced by the 'Big Bang' de-regulation of the financial markets, and the development of London as one of the small number of world financial centres along with New York and Tokyo.

4.29 The picture sketched above draws heavily upon a number of useful studies of producer services published in the last few years by the **Leyshon, Daniels and Thrift** team. They studied each of the main groups within the producer services 'sector', looking at the impact of the rapid concentration of ownership and control, and the importance of takeovers and mergers, innovations and technological change. The pivotal role of the City of London emerges from their studies, but at the same time certain provincial cities such as Manchester have seen a major growth in both banking (there are now 60 foreign banks with offices in Manchester) and business services. While there are many possibilities for the decentralisation of producer services in the future, there are other processes (such as the use of fibre optics in telecommunications) which will reinforce centralisation. One of the products of this research is a view of London as an 'outlier' in Britain, increasingly linked to other world cities through its international connections, and to a certain extent cut off from the rest of Britain, with its house prices, for example, boosted by the housing needs of its many new international migrants such as foreign bank employees.

4(ix) Flexibility; new forms of work organisation; self-employment

4.30 A major theme in recent research is that the developments in the geography of employment and trends towards a deindustrialisation of the economies of the West are connected with epochal structural changes in economic life. These structural changes have been conceptualised in various ways. One view is that western economies and societies are moving into a post-industrial stage. Others draw on the work of Kondratief, Schumpeter and Freeman to argue that capitalist industrialisation goes through fifty-year cycles. The 1960s and 1970s represent one such turning point as an earlier industrial paradigm goes into crisis and a new one emerges. In the recent period, however, the ideas of the French 'regulation' school have become increasingly popular. Economic development is studied with the aid of concepts such as 'industrial paradigm', 'mode of regulation' and 'regime of accumulation': a socio-institutional structure or matrix within which accumulation occurs, made up of market mechanisms, institutions, social relationships, and state intervention. Fordism is one such regime of accumulation.

4.33 Underlying Fordism in the early post-war decades were high volume production, a rapid growth in the productivity of labour, and substantial reductions in the unit value of commodities. Wages increased in line with productivity. With rising real incomes and changes in the mode of consumption in favour of the products of the new industries, demand increased and reinforced the expansion of production capacity, while investments in new capacity fuelled the demand for capital equipment. As a result, mass consumption emerged as a corollary of mass production, and the conditions of life of large sections of the skilled and unskilled working class as well as of middle strata were transformed.

4.34 The Fordist model of development, however, partially broke down during the 1970s, to be replaced, according to some accounts, by 'flexible specialisation'. The flexibility comes from the use of automation, and from the use of labour in new ways, and the specialisation comes from the orientation of production towards smaller niche markets. Production can therefore be adapted more quickly to technological uncertainty and volatility of demand.

4.35 It is claimed that these changes helped to bring about a new industrial structure. In areas where flexible specialisation came to prevail new types of inter-firm relations and a new kind of industrial structure composed of a network of small and medium sized firms often became predominant. Large establishments were closed or were reorganised with much smaller workforces, and activities or phases of work that formerly took place in large factories were transferred to small and medium sized firms or were put out to domestic workers. Both self-employment and small firms have indeed tended to increase in the UK in the recent period.

4.36 Increased flexibility was also sought in the workplace. Two main kinds of flexibility are involved. One is functional flexibility which refers to the capacity of a firm to adjust the tasks performed by workers it employs according to changes in demand, technology, or marketing policy. This kind of flexibility is achieved mainly through the recruitment of a group of polyvalent core workers with multiple and transferable skills. The second is numerical flexibility. Numerical flexibility refers to the ease and speed with which firms can adjust the number of workers employed to meet fluctuations in demand. In addition, employers seek financial flexibility in the form of a capacity to alter the structure of pay according to the level of employment and the type of work each worker is doing and through moving towards local pay bargaining.

4.37 Those who advocate the use of the flexible specialisation approach argue that as a result of the strategy of seeking functional and numerical flexibility, the segmentation of the working population into core and peripheral workers has been reinforced. Included in the peripheral category are two groups of people. One is composed of the workers employed by subcontractors, specialised self-employed workers, and staff supplied by temporary employment agencies. The second is made up of some of the firm's own employees. Included in this group are workers without career status who can be laid off or re-employed according to economic conditions, workers with temporary contracts of employment, part-time and casual staff, and people in groups with a high turnover whose numbers can easily be réduced by a policy of non-replacement. As a result the dualism in the market for labour has increased. The size of the core working population has declined, while temporary and irregular jobs on the one hand, and moonlighting or second jobs on the other have proliferated. With these developments and with the division of the working class that they imply, the strength of the working class movement has been undermined.

4.38 Few seem to doubt that one of the most important elements in urban change in the UK in recent years has been this transformation of work implied by the partial replacement of Fordist forms of production by flexible specialisation. Two problems arise, however. The first is that despite the considerable research effort referred to above, the geographical pattern of these new work practises are at present very incompletely known and understood. 'Japanisation' (in an extremely dilute form) is evident in parts of North East

England and South Wales, and small firm growth and self-employment are particularly well developed in parts of southern Britain, but it is probably too early as yet to see the urban and regional aspects of changes such as the moves towards single-union, no-strike deals, or the use of CAD/CAM (computer aided design/computer assisted manufacturing) in manufacturing industry. The second problem is conceptual; the term 'flexible specialisation' has come to be used to cover a range of changes which is far too inclusive — changes in the labour process, in industrial structure, in industrial relations and in the use of technology. This has resulted in something of a reaction against the use of concepts such as 'flexibility' or 'post-Fordism'. **Pollert** (1987), for example, develops the argument that there is nothing new about calls for greater flexibility in the workplace; what is new is the ideological force and content of the call for greater flexibility in 1980s Britain. In comparison with this, the changes which have actually taken place are fairly minor, often involving an increase in subcontracting arrangements, and do not add up to the model 'flexible firm' as described by Atkinson and his colleagues at the Institute of Manpower Studies. Pollert is particularly scathing about the assumption in the flexibility literature that the security of 'core' workers has become enhanced by these changes. Others castigate those who herald the end of Fordism, and who point to the 'Third Italy' as a model for future small-firm based, high-technology, spatially decentralised production in Britain. They argue that mass (?Fordist) production is alive and well, and flourishing in Japan, where culture-related differences in industrial organisation have permitted the highly efficient production of consumer goods for the export market. It is this, above all, that has then forced UK producers to seek new market niches, new inter- and intra-firm relations, and new methods of production. Like Pollert, these authors dismiss much of the literature on flexible specialisation as 'hype', and label some of the visions of post-Fordism (such as that of Sabel and Piore in their 'Work and Politics') as 'sentimental'.

4(x) Youth labour markets; training and recruitment; early retirement

4.39   In the last section there was some discussion (conducted at the general level) of labour market segmentation. In this and the next two sections we review literature on the segmentation of labour markets on the basis of age, sex and ethnicity.

4.40   It is clear that as urban employment opportunities decreased during the 1970s, and decreased even more rapidly in the period 1979–83, the burden fell very predominantly on the young person and young adult, and secondarily upon those who were approaching the end of their working lives. Some of this latter group (mostly men) were able to choose, or were constrained to take, early retirement, some of the young people stayed on in full-time education, and some women gave up the search for employment and concentrated on domestic labour, but most of those without work became part of the three million unemployed.

4.41   Youth unemployment rates in the 1980s were particularly high in the main industrial conurbations of northern and western Britain and in the West Midlands. They were lowest in the towns and rural areas around London and in freestanding towns in southern England. So great were the differences in youth unemployment rates that a young person leaving school in St. Albans, Hertfordshire had a one in forty chance of failing to obtain employment in 1983, whereas for a young person in Sunderland the rate was between one in three and one in four. These figures come from a study by **Ashton, Maguire and Spilsbury** (1988) in which they report the results of research on the significance of local labour markets for the life chances of young people. On the basis of surveys carried out in Leicester, St Albans, Stafford and Sunderland, they argue that local labour markets not only affect the chances of obtaining a job, but also the type of job (three times as many males entered professional, managerial and technical work in St Albans than in Sunderland), the likelihood of job change (much higher in the St Albans), and length of period of unemployment (much higher in Sunderland). They also show that these labour market differences affect work attitudes. In St Albans attitudes to school and education were far more positive than in Sunderland or Stafford. In part this was because the kinds of jobs available locally called for educational qualifications, whereas those in the North did not. In contrast, the young people in Sunderland were very fatalistic in their attitudes and saw little point in obtaining additional skills through training courses. Ashton, Maguire and Spilsbury found that these results were not due to the social class differences between the places; working class young people in St Albans had distinctly better life chances than those in Sunderland.

4(xi) Jobs and gender; 'feminisation' in local labour markets

4.42   Two of the best known facts about urban employment change in the recent period are:

(i) that there has been a significant increase in the proportion of the total workforce that is female; and

(ii) that the urban and regional differences in the proportions of women in the economically active age-groups who are 'economically active' have narrowed appreciably. The female activity rates of many industrial towns and cities and most rural areas, which previously lagged well behind those of the commercial cities, and, above all London, increased more rapidly than the average to produce a convergence of rates around the national figure.

4.43   How could this increase in, and spatial convergence of, rates come about? There are many possible mechanisms at work. Firstly, it is possible that there have been differences in the rates of growth or decline of occupations and sectors employing men, and those employing women. For example, in the 1960s and early 1970s there was a rapid expansion of certain kinds of public sector service employment (health and education services in particular) which had a high propensity to employ women. Similarly, during the late 1970s and early 1980s there were very many redundancies in manufacturing industry where skilled manual labour was predominantly male. A second way in which this increase in female employment could have taken place is through a strict substitution of women for men in the workplace. The evidence of this is almost non-existent, which, given the high degree of gender segregation in employment, is hardly surprising. 'Feminisation' in this sense, therefore, has not occurred to any appreciable extent in the recent period. Thirdly, there might be changes in gender relations in the household which affect women's ability to take up paid employment. Specifically, birth rates in the UK declined steadily between 1965 and the late 1970s, and as the time between the first and last child was reduced so the period of maximum domestic responsibilities for women with children was also diminished. At the same time marriage rates declined and childlessness in marriage increased. Finally, the increase might be regarded as more illusory than real since this period saw a big increase in part-time employment, and part-time jobs are overwhelmingly carried out by women.

4.44   The literature on gender relations and the restructuring process is now expanding fast. Some of the literature is fairly general and conceptual; other studies focus on the changes taking place in particular localities. In addition to the interest in part-time employment (90% female) there is an awareness that, although there is a little homeworking carried out by professional men, most of the homeworking is done by women. The rapid increase in married women's activity rates has also provoked a research interest in the dual earning (two career) household. One of the problems facing such households is their interest in (or dependence upon) finding two jobs. This is one of the many instances where gender and class interconnect; social class inequalities may be intensifying as rising female employment participation, resulting in dual career patterns, become much more common among middle-class and upper middle-class couples. Dual income patterns are also increasingly common in working class

households — with both men and women engaging in paid work but in relatively disadvantaged labour market positions. However, the gap in income and job security between working class men and women persists with working class women segregated into the worst jobs of all.

4.45   This last point raises the general issue of perspective in studies of gender relations in urban employment change. Feminist authors stress the problem of taking for granted what has to be explained, namely patriarchal gender relations, both inside the home and in employment, which structure women's access to jobs. Any consideration of the changing participation of women in the paid workforce can only be understood in this context.

4(xii)   Race and employment; immigrant workers

4.46   The problem with reviewing the literature on labour market segmentation in the way adopted here (that is, first age, then sex, then race) is that attention is diverted away from the manner in which these divisions interconnect, often in such a way as to compound the effects of disadvantage.

4.47   One theme which has received attention from both economists and sociologists is the income differential between black workers and white workers in contemporary Britain. The implications of this difference for an understanding of urban change is that black households are overwhelmingly concentrated in the main urban areas and in the inner parts of those areas. The research focus is often upon racism and how it affects recruitment, both generally, and in specific instances, but there are also empirical studies, using sources such as the General Household Survey, of the degree of earnings differentials between black and white employees, and research which shows that journey to work distances are greater for black workers than for equivalent white workers. Many studies focus on the problems of access to employment and training experienced by young blacks.

4.48   Cross and Johnson provide data on the labour market positions of different ethnic groups in inner city locations in the West Midlands (**Cross and Johnson 1988**). They show that 'Afro-Caribbean' men obtain the lowest wages, and that household incomes (standardised for size) are lower for 'Asians' and Afro-Caribbeans than for whites. They argue that the original reasons for these differences lie in the migrant labour status of the workers, but that disadvantage has been sustained by racial exclusion. They reject suggestions that disadvantage arises from inappropriate skills or aspirations, or from under-achievement in the educational system. Racial exclusion operates, they claim, both at the recruitment stage and in the processes of selection and promotion internal to organizations. They point out that part of the problem is that, due to their spatial concentration, ethnic minorities are now totally dependent upon the fortunes of inner city economies, which have declined significantly in the period since the migrants arrived there in the 1950s to the early 1970s. Cross and Johnson then examine three aspects of social mobility: the level of entry to the labour market; intra-generational mobility; and inter-generational mobility. They find that disadvantage is marked at entry, and is not explainable in terms of social class background; that ethnic minorities experience more downward intra-generational mobility than whites, but that black women are more upwardly mobile intra-generationally than black men; and that ethnic differences in inter-generational mobility are very great, with only a quarter of Afro-Caribbean men achieving upward mobility, where the figure for whites is over half. The authors conclude by saying that the workers were unable to use migration as a lever for inter-generational improvement, hence the 'Lost Illusions' of the title of the book.

Evaluation

4.49   This has necessarily been a long Chapter encompassing a wide range of research initiatives. It has not been easy, therefore, to select a conveniently small number of conclusions. However, the following comments record our judgements in relation to the issues raised at the beginning of the Chapter:

(i) employment declined in every major city in the 1970s (including London) and in most cities in the 1980s. This decline was largely due to a process of deindustrialisation;

(ii) urban manufacturing employment decline cannot be understood satisfactorily using a 'location factors' approach; instead, it is necessary to relate job loss to a reorganisation of production which occurred within an increasingly international economic order;

(iii) the burden of manufacturing job loss fell disproportionately upon young people and black people. It affected both men and women. Women were major beneficiaries of the many new jobs created in the services during the recent period. A high proportion of these jobs were, however, part-time and insecure in nature. Despite the fact that an overall decline in male employment coincided with an increase in female employment, one should avoid the use of the term 'feminisation' to describe this process, since this is often quite mistakenly interpreted to mean that there was a direct substitution of women for men in particular jobs;

(iv) disadvantages relating to class, gender and race tend to interact and to reinforce one another;

(v) the most significant aspect of the growth of the service sector was the expansion of 'producer services'. This affected several major provincial cities, but it was most crucial in altering the employment situation in London, particularly in the early-mid 1980s;

(vi) as a result of this, and of the location of high technology firms and back offices in other areas of southern and south eastern England, there has been a re-emergence of the north-south divide in the geography of employment;

(vii) there is some substance in the notion of 'flexible specialisation', and some features of its geography are beginning to emerge. However, the claims that Fordist forms of mass-production have been replaced by the work practices of the 'flexible firm' are at least premature, and probably unfounded. Furthermore, the image of an autonomous, private sector, small firm-based, high technology growth zone located around and to the west of London must be tempered by an awareness of the international peripherality of this area, and of the important degree to which these developments have been linked to UK defence procurement, and to public sector investment in transport infrastructure and research laboratories.

The influence of economic and technological change on the urban system and on urban built form

Issues

5.1   This Chapter reviews research which traces the effects of changes in the sphere of work upon the nature of the UK urban system and of its built form character.

The main issues raised in this Chapter are:

(i) in what ways and to what degree have the changes which have been witnessed in the structure of the UK urban system, and of cities within that system, been due to the adoption of new technologies in production and circulation, and of the widespread use of the products of these new technologies in everyday life? Is there empirical substance to concepts such as 'Silicon Landscapes' or to the geography of an 'Information Economy'?

(ii) can one argue that the nature of urban built form change in the UK in the recent period has been shaped by processes specific to the construction and house-building industries? If so, how, and why, and to what effect?

(iii) how has the changing geography of employment influenced population redistribution in the recent period? More specifically, how have these employment changes affected local housing markets and the nature of urban built form? Much more generally, has there been a sea-change in the nature of capitalist production sufficient to manifest itself in a 'postmodern' form of urbanisation?

Contributions

5(i) **The impact of technological change on the urban system; the information economy**

5.2   The literature on urban change in the UK contains many references to the importance of technology. There is a widespread sense, both in academic circles and in the media, that we have been passing through a period of accelerated change in our working lives and at home brought on by the spread of new technologies, particularly, but not exclusively, in the form of products which use micro-electronics. In its crudest form this perception is incorporated into a technological determinism — that is to say, a view of social and economic change which is 'read off' from technological change. In such an approach human history is seen as the outcome of scientific discoveries and technological achievements; the steam engine set in motion the industrialisation and urbanisation of the nineteenth century, just as the telephone, television, motor car and jumbo jet command social relations today (and space technologies will determine the societies of the future).

5.3   Some argue that through the purchase of technologically sophisticated products such as cars, washing machines, television sets and home computers, services previously provided by the market economy or by the public sector, can be transferred into the domestic sphere to bolster the 'self-service economy'. It is not in the domestic sphere, however, that technology is seen to be having its greatest impact on our cities and regions. Rather it is through automation, seen as a response to economic crisis, and applied to improve the productivity of labour, the quality and reliability of the products, and the efficiency of the whole production process. Automation, and new technologies such as bio-technology can, it is claimed, alter the geography of production and the distribution of employment opportunities.

5.4   The most important contributions to our understanding of the spatial impacts of technological change emanate from the CURDS group at Newcastle University. To examine the CURDS work on technological change and the urban system we can select a couple of papers which are fairly representative of recent work carried out at the Centre. The first, by **Goddard and Gillespie** (1987), considers the urban and regional implications of recent developments in information and telecommunications technology. They begin by arguing that as the generation, processing and exchange of information becomes a larger part of total economic activity, technical developments affecting this activity also increase in significance. Telecommunications, as the 'electronic highways of the future' will influence the geography of economic activity 'as much as the railways did in earlier periods of profound structural change'. They point out that the determinant of the effects of the new technologies in an 'information economy' will be the patterns of access to information. The new technologies might permit wider access, thus spreading the benefits more broadly. What they fear, however, is that, in practice, the information economy will be neither equitable nor efficient due to the increasing privatisation or commodification of information, and to its increasing control by transnational corporations. They base their fears upon what has already happened in the realm of telecommunications. Firstly, there is a regional imbalance in the distribution of 'information workers', with London and the South East leading and the Northern and Western regions lagging behind. Exacerbating this imbalance is the fact that the quality of these jobs is generally higher in London and the South East. Secondly, the introduction of new telecommunications technology is spatially uneven, with London and a small number of major provincial cities being served first, thus endowing firms located there with a competitive advantage over firms in other places. For example, London is already well ahead in terms of telephone and telex subscribers per 100 inhabitants. This advantageous position is reinforced by the costs of using the services; a firm in the South East can contact a third of all business telephones in the UK at the cost of a local call — the equivalent figure for Newcastle is 1%!

5.5   Some of these arguments reappear in the paper by **Robins and Hepworth** (1988), but in this case the intention is rather broader: it is to speculate on the nature of urbanisation in an 'information economy'. The authors begin by castigating both technological determinism, and the style of popular writing which predicts, and eulogises, the coming of the 'electronic cottage' and the 'smart' home. They call for an understanding of the new technologies which place them in the context of important transformations in the nature of capitalist societies. These transformations are then described using the concepts of Fordism (see 4(ix) above) and neo-Fordism (where this is seen as roughly equivalent to 'flexible specialisation' see 4.34 above). The overcoming of physical geography (dis-

tance etc) and the constraints of time (duration, sequence, 'natural' time rhythms) under neo-Fordism leads to a new fluidity in location, and to a flexibility in the use of time. The rest of the paper consists of speculations about the impact of 'home interactive telematics', on 'economic life', 'politics and power', and 'surveillance and regulation'. Under the heading of economic life, the shift to homeworking is emphasised, and its likely (often detrimental) affects on household social relations is traced. This shift reduces workplace organisation (trade unionism) and promotes a casualisation of the workforce. The importance of changes in consumption, notably through teleshopping is also stressed. The authors expect the urban system to alter its spatial structure as a result of these changes, in particular, major cities will concede much of their importance to motorway intersections and to the urbanised countryside, and the north and west will lose out to the south and east. In so far as the city itself is affected, it will see the creation of 'electronic skyscraper fortresses cordoned off from depleted and decaying inner city areas'. This will partly reflect the re-concentration of certain economic activities in the city, and, in particular, of information-based activities in the so-called global cities (e.g. London, New York, Tokyo).

5.6   Home information telematics will also affect politics and power. Robins and Hepworth claim that new technology facilitates a recapitalisaton (privatisation) of activities previously carried out in the public domain (for example health, education and media services) (see section 3(iv) above). Accompanied by a centralisation of power, this privatisation will lead to a weakening of collective action, and of 'local and civic cultural identity'. Thus the 'information city' threatens to be a 'segmented, segregated, atomised place', divided into 'antagonistic spaces, with expensive safe places and cheap unsafe places'. The basis of individual identity will be the home, with the city ceasing to be a unit of social interaction or of identification. But life in these pod-like homes will not be idyllic; there will be a further penetration of individual privacy as 'the household becomes increasingly transparent, subject to electronic scrutiny and cognitive intrusion'. Clearly, this picture of the information city is not an attractive one and it contrasts sharply with the utopian visions of many of the propagandists of both the new technologies, and of the related changes in attitudes and industrial organisation (e.g. the entreprenurial culture and small-firm growth) which accompany them.

5(ii) The role of the construction industry and of the housebuilding system in shaping urban development

5.7   A second way in which relationships in the sphere of work and employment can impact on the urban

34

system is through the effects that the construction industry can have on the nature of urban built form. The argument here is that needs and demands for housing and for infrastructure are mediated by the opportunities offered, and constraints imposed, by that branch of production which serves to meet these demands — the construction/housebuilding industry. How the built form of urban areas actually changes is therefore a product of the interaction of demand and supply, with the latter shaping the former as well as responding to it. That there is no automatic adjustment of supply of urban built form to meet demand has already been referred to in another section of this report (section 2(iv)). For example, the potential for rapid social and economic change in the Docklands area of London has existed for a long time, it took the investment decisions of a number of major companies to alter expectations, and the subsequent changes have reflected the structures and relations of the property development industry. An obvious point to be made about the activities of the construction industry is that in the recent period (and especially since 1979) there has been a major shift away from construction for service towards construction for profit. This is not only true for consumption-related products such as houses and leisure complexes, but also for service spaces such as offices, and for infrastructure investments (such as the Channel Tunnel). At the same time there has been a sharp reduction in the amount of construction carried out by the public sector, as Direct Labour Organisations have been run down. Also, with the sale of council houses (and now of whole estates), there has been a transfer of maintenance building work into the private sector. One of the other significant aspects of this change is that a spatial standardisation of output arising from the application of bureaucratic rules has been partially replaced by investments which reflect perceived profit potential, and which have tended, therefore to be spatially more selective.

5.8 A recent study by **Dickens et al.** (1985) addresses this issue of the role of the housebuilders and developers in shaping the changing nature of British cities. Part of their study consists of a comparative analysis of housing construction in Britain and Sweden. The purpose of this is to demonstrate the distinctiveness of the British land development and housing system, and the importance of production relationships in determining housing outcomes.

5.9 They criticise the view that because of their bulk, the need for complex integration of tasks on site, the need for craft work, and the complication of land development profits, building houses will always suffer from low productivity, with low levels of mechanisation and capitalisation — implying that houses will be built by out-moded technology and in small numbers, and be sold at high prices. The basis of their criticism is that in Sweden, a profitable, private sector housebuilding

industry is based upon a very different kind of production system. The process is highly capital-intensive, involves production of whole sections of the house in the factory rather than on site, uses high productivity labour, and gains almost no profits from the land price increases which accompany development.

5.10 The reason for the differences are to be found in the legal, historical and institutional contexts of the housebuilding process. While Sweden, like Britain (until recently) has a large social housing sector, most private sector housing is not built speculatively as in Britain. Rather, private sector builders are subject to local authority contracts stipulating the nature, timing and price of new dwellings, and use land from local authority owned land banks. In return, builders have access to subsidised loans. The interests of Swedish housebuilders are hence directed towards maintaining competitiveness by achieving efficiency in the production of housing, rather than, as in Britain, seeking windfall land development profits and speculative price gains. This results in a 'virtuous circle' in Sweden of capitalisation, labour process rationalisation and technical innovation, compared to Britain's 'vicious circle' of low capitalisation, fewer economies of scale, low productivity and inadequate training, where profits can be found outside the production process itself. The result is that British homes are of a poorer quality and higher relative price in a more market-dominated economy, while in Sweden new dwellings are both higher quality and relatively cheaper, produced by capitalist building companies which are particularly efficient because of wide-ranging state intervention.

5.11 The policy implications of this research on the housebuilding industry in Britain are very considerable. The British housebuilding industry appears to be less efficient than those of certain other Western European countries and is more concerned with land value appreciation as a source of profit. If the present land development and housebuilding system produces over-expensive houses on over-valued land, then the potential to solve the housing problems of low income households is very severely restricted.

5(iii) **Labour market influences on housing and built form; economic restructuring and the urban system**

5.12 The final section of this Chapter reviews research which is concerned with the manner and degree to which the housing and built form characteristics of cities and regions are a product of the changes taking place in the sphere of work and employment relations. These labour market/housing market relations have already been referred to in an earlier section of this report (2(i)), but there the emphasis was on the influence of housing markets on labour markets; here the reverse causality is the focus of interest.

5.13 One of the key factors influencing urban change is investment in housing, and the level of investment is closely related to the job market position of the residents. Building societies are most inclined to lend to people who have secure, well-paid employment, with good promotion prospects in areas where such people tend to dominate. The process is, of course, circular; those who have obtained mortgage finance for house purchase, are in a privileged position in the labour market, since they can afford to be geographically mobile, and can use their property as collateral for many purposes including entry into self-employment. Circularity also exists at an aggregate level because those areas which have seen the most rapid increase in house prices and mortgage debt, have also witnessed the largest increases in land and property-related financial and business service employment. Thus the South of England has attracted vast sums of mortgage debt because of the buoyancy of its labour market. At the same time, many of the jobs created by that debt accrue to the south of England because of the concentration there of producer services employment.

5.14 Recent research on housing and labour markets in specific localities reveals the complex interdependencies between them. Thus **Barlow and Savage** (1986) in their study of Berkshire point to the fact that housing demand was heightened by the continuous growth of employment in this favoured part of the British sunbelt during the 1970s and 1980s. Much of this growth was in the services (especially in producer services), but, by the early 1980s, a sizeable 10% of the workforce was employed in high-technology industries. very little of the employment growth, however, matched the skills of those being released by the employment decline of 'Fordist' consumer-goods industries (such as car parts and confectionery). This has meant that unemployment has co-existed with severe shortages of highly-skilled labour.

5.15 The implications of this situation are that those being made redundant, or for whom job opportunities are decreasing, are thereby weakened in their ability to compete in a housing market which is increasingly dominated by the needs of the high paid members of the service class, attracted to the area by the new jobs in producer services and high technology industry. These latter incomers are assisted in their ability to out-bid locals by the relocation packages often negotiated with their new employers.

5.16 Barlow and Savage show that during the period of job growth the housing stock also expanded, but that this expansion took the form of expensive houses, speculatively built by the volume housebuilders on

estates, often after central government had overturned the refusal of planning permission for development issued by the local council. Two-thirds of the purchasers of these houses were professional or managerial workers, and their incomes were 25% above the average for the purchasers of new houses in the South East region. Not surprisingly, house prices increased rapidly, and with high levels of council house sales, the availability of housing for those on lower incomes became very restricted, and many young people have been effectively shut out of the local housing market altogether.

5.17 These high prices, boosted by strong anti-growth coalitions against land release for new housing, have hit local employers, who are finding it increasingly difficult to house their workforces, both their professional employees and their skilled manual workers. Barlow and Savage conclude by asserting that, 'in Berkshire there seems to be a two-way relationship between the housing market and labour market: the structure of the labour market influences the price of, and demand for, housing in a given area; and the resulting forms of housing provision make it difficult to recruit non-professional workers from outside the area and influence the structure of the workforce' (for example, by putting extra pressure on women to work in order to meet the high housing costs).

5.18 Finally, a lot of interest has been generated recently by attempts to examine the relations between economy and space at a much more general level. Some have claimed, for example, that there are connections between regimes of accumulation (Fordism/flexible specialisation) on the one hand, and styles of architecture and urban design (Modern/post-Modern) on the other. The central idea is that the kinds of production and consumption which typified the 'regime of accumulation' called 'Fordism' (mass production, especially assembly-line production of standardised goods for mass markets), are realised in the urban landscapes of that period — the low density housing estate mostly for owner-occupation, and high-rise council flats. The suburb is then seen as the physical manifestation of the social phenomenon of the 'mass collective worker'; its architecture and design are functional, technocratic, managerial and banal. After about 1973, as Fordism becomes partially replaced by post-Fordism (flexible specialisation), the new urban landscapes are to be found not so much in the suburbs, but back in the inner, or even the central city, or conversely, outside the city altogether. The scale of urban development now becomes smaller, and its built form is much more varied. The social content of this urban development also changes; the new and renovated housing is for wealthier people — the growing service class, and the small employers and self-employed. Thus the location and physical character of new urban development is, according to this approach, interpretable in the light of changes in the nature of the economic system, acting partly through the social class realignment that these changes imply (see Section 8.1 below).

Evaluation

5.19   Our judgments in relation to this literature are as follows:

(i) that, despite the progress made in relating advanced telecommunications to corporate power, and on documenting the centralising tendencies of information technology, the literature in this field still suffers from an overly abstract and unexamined concept of 'information'. Abstracting 'information' from the contexts and purposes for which it is used tends to gloss over the differences between information, knowledge and skills, and between information processing and problem-solving. In our judgment the role of information technology in the latter is minor, and the need for face-to-face contact for problem-solving remains as strong as ever. Thus much of the literature overestimates the possibilities for decentralisation;

(ii) that there is considerable evidence to support the view that post-1970 urban development in the UK has been greatly affected by the nature of the construction industry itself — its organisation, methods of financing and production technology, and its situation within the planning and land development system; and

(iii) that labour market changes have greatly influenced the location, pace and content of urban development in the recent period. In particular, the redistribution of population in the 1970s largely reflects the emergence of a 'new geography of production', following the weakening of regional sectoral specialisation and the development of a new, or hierarchical, division of labour (see Section 9(v)) each occurring within Fordist forms of production and consumption. At the same time, however, the idea that the built form character of urban development has been shaped since then by the erosion of Fordist forms of production and the enhancement of tendencies towards 'flexible specialisation' has proved highly provocative, and is likely to attract much attention in the future.

CHAPTER 6

The impact of employment change on social life

6.1 In the early 1980s urban and regional research was mostly focused on the nature of the economic changes which were taking place in the major cities of the UK, and, in particular, in their inner areas. Subsequently, attention shifted somewhat towards the impacts of these changes on the lives of the people living in these areas, for example through factory closures and high levels of youth and long-term unemployment. In this Chapter we review the literature on the social effects of economic restructuring, both at a general level and at the level of specific localities.

Issues

6.2 Four main issues can be identified in the literature:

(i) the first is summed up in the title of the first publication from the ESRC's Changing Urban and Regional System Initiative, 'Global Restructuring, Local Response' (Cooke [ed] 1986). What have been the impacts on specific localities of global level economic changes (notably industrial restructuring)? And how have local factors meshed with these global factors to produce particular outcomes? Research on this theme has resulted in the development of a new approach — 'locality research' — that is, the intensive study of sub-regional areas to investigate how global and local forces interact;

(ii) more specifically, what has been the impact of economic change, acting through local labour markets, upon local class structures? What have been the social effects of labour market processes such as those described by the concepts of 'flexibility', 'deskilling' and 'feminisation'? And have these changes in local

labour markets affected local politics and party political support? And

(iii) how have employment changes altered household relations? Do rising male unemployment and increased female participation in the labour market challenge traditional gender roles? How do households cope with unemployment?

Contributions

6(i) **The role of economic restructuring in urban and regional social change; locality studies (general, that is, not location-specific)**

6.3 It is now almost universally accepted that changes in the UK economy in the 1970s and 1980s have, through their effects on work and employment, resulted in increases in social inequality. There is not only evidence of widening differences between different social groups at the national level, but also signs of a social polarisation between north and south, between the industrial city and the urbanised country-side, and between the inner city, the outer council estates and the rest of the urban area.

6.4 The work of **Lash and Urry** has been particularly influential in this field (Lash and Urry 1987). In a book which is a rich source of ideas about economic and social change in western societies, they argue that the transition from 'organised' to 'disorganised' capitalism experienced in the UK over the last twenty years implies a fragmentation of workforces into smaller establishments in more spatially dispersed locations, each displaying more diversified industrial and occupational structures. This reduces worker organisation and class solidarity, and leads to class dealignment in politics, and to an increase in cultural fragmentation and pluralism.

6.5 This emphasis on the ways in which economic restructuring generates poverty in the inner city and in industrial towns and regions, has a long history. It constituted, for example, a central theme of the Community Development Project (CDP) studies on the 'costs of industrial change' published in the mid to late 1970s. These studies drew attention to the broader international and national economic contexts of the changes being experienced by people living in these areas, and in particular to the social implications of external control, and of labour market segmentation. Above all, social changes in specific localities were interpreted as being the product of the managerial strategies of firms, which generate poverty by offering jobs with poor or uncertain rewards, bad conditions and little training, or by withdrawing jobs altogether from the area. The stimulus to this work on managerial strategies came from Braverman's influential 'Labour and Monopoly Capital', but its incorporation into our understanding of the problems of urban poverty in Britain was largely due to the work of the CDP teams.

6.6 The CDPs may have set the agenda for discussions about the local effects of global restructuring, but the direction of this line of research has recently been dominated by the team, headed by **Phil Cooke** at UWIST, working on the ESRC's 'Changing Urban and Regional System' (CURS) Initiative. The CURS project, begun in October 1984, grew out of ideas developed by Doreen Massey who saw a need for a research focus on the changes taking place in specific localities. This would reveal the ways that global economic restructuring processes were interacting with the social structures and relations of particular places to produce actual outcomes (such as job losses or gains, changes in people's lifestyles and attitudes, etc).

6.7 Localities with contrasting economic profiles were chosen in order to show the variety of local responses possible in the face of divergent forms of economic restructuring. The seven localities chosen were Middlesbrough, outer Liverpool and southwest Birmingham (depressed areas which had suffered from branch plant closures), Cheltenham and Swindon (chosen because they were more prosperous and were benefiting from the decentralisation of service employment), and two 'hybrid' localities, Thanet (which was an economically depressed area in the generally prosperous South East region), and Lancaster (a locality apparently able to expand its service employment to offset its losses in manufacturing.

6.8 The teams adopted a labour market-led approach since this allowed them to draw upon the conceptua-

lisation available in the spatial divisions of labour/industrial restructuring literature. Each locality team carried out a questionnaire survey of 'target' groups, that is, those people most likely to be affected by restructuring. They also interviewed the major employers in the locality, plus trade union officials and local policy-makers (officers and politicians).

6.9 The key themes in locality change identified by the CURS research are, firstly, those which relate to the restructuring process, notably the internationalisation of the economy, the trend towards flexibility, and the 'feminisation' of the workforce. Secondly, the trend towards privatisation, both in the housing market and as a general phenomenon. Thirdly, political change, not just as reflected in election results, but in the shift of power away from the blue-collar unions towards the white-collar ones. Fourthly, social polarisation especially associated with the growth of the service class. Fifthly, local cultures, which vary considerably between the case studies. Finally, local effectivity. This last idea has been given considerable prominence in the CURS work. It claims that all localities contain the capacity to become 'proactive', that is, to take fate into their own hands and to act to shape the future of their locality. Local effectivity is not equivalent to what the local authority does, though place marketing (boosterism) does sometimes happen. Rather it is people organising themselves around the locality itself as a base.

6.10 In a remarkable convergence of research interests, at about the same time as the geographers, economists and planners were setting up the CURS initiative, the ERSC was being pressed hard by its sociologists for a major empirical study, involving local case studies, of the changes in social attitudes and behaviours accompanying, and consequent upon, the important changes in work and employment which had taken place in the 1980s. The outcome of this pressure was the establishment in 1985 of the 'Social Change and Economic Life' (SCEL) Initiative co-ordinated by **Duncan Gallie** from Nuffield College, Oxford.

6.11 The broad outlines of the SCEL initiative are clearly presented in Gallie (1985). There are four main research areas:

(i) the nature and determinants of employer labour force strategies;

(ii) the character and direction of change in worker attitudes to employment and the labour market;

(iii) the changing dynamics of household relations and their implications for both paid and unpaid work; and

(iv) the impact of changes in employment structure on social integration and social stratification.

Six localities were chosen for detailed study, primarily on the basis of contrasting unemployment levels and recent employment histories: Aberdeen, Swindon and Northampton had relatively low levels of unemployment, unlike Coventry, Kirkaldy and Rochdale which had unemployment rates well above the national average. A major part of the SCEL effort consists of a survey of 1000 adults in each locality. Two thirds of the questionnaire is common to all localities so that full comparability can be achieved. Much of this survey is concerned with work attitudes and in obtaining information on work histories. In addition, each locality study includes a survey of 300 establishments to provide the information on employer labour force strategies. A follow-up study of 300 adults, drawn from the 1000 people interviewed in the work attitudes survey, provides information on family value systems, the organisation of unpaid work and the nature of household work strategies. While much of the work is common to each of the six locality teams, there are many team-specific projects, and three additional studies which do not relate to specific places.

6.12 Although many research papers arising from CURS and SCEL have been written, the results of the initiatives are only now beginning to appear in published form. It is impossible, therefore, to evaluate these initiatives at this stage, and difficult to assess the relations between SCEL and CURS. While they both investigate the impact of employment change on social relationships, the specific topics of interest differ somewhat, with SCEL devoting much more effort to changing work attitudes, for example. The use of the locality studies is also different. SCEL does not seem to share CURS's interest in the way in which the economic, the social and the political connect (or do not connect) with one another at the level of the individual locality, and there is no SCEL equivalent to the CURS emphasis on local pro-activity. The purpose of the locality studies in SCEL seems to be rather more 'traditional'; it is to provide evidence of specific instances to support generalisations about economic and social change at the level of British society as a whole.

6(ii) Studies in specific localities of the social effects of economic restructuring

6.13 Not surprisingly, many locality studies have been carried out in the West Midlands, and in the two regions of northern England where industrial decline has most transformed the local economies. The North East figured in the CDP programme, in the Inner Cities Research Programme where Newcastle was chosen for the policy evaluation case study, and in the CURS initiative where Middlesbrough is the locality in question. This latter research continues important work carried out at Durham University on the way industrial investment, followed by disinvestment and

redundancy were experienced by ordinary working people in the North East region in the late 1960s and 1970s. The North West region was not represented in ICRP but it figures prominantly in CURS and SCEL. The CURS programme has two localities in the region; the first is the home town of the Lancaster Regionalism Group, and the second is Liverpool. In this case the focus of attention has been the large peripheral council estates, where **Richard Meegan** has been studying responses to unemployment. He argues that these responses are only understandable in the light of the recent employment history of Merseyside. Casualised dock labour and routinised jobs in Fordist factories led to an expectation of job insecurity, a fatalism and a belligerency towards employers. Yet it also produced a certain vitality. This manifests itself most visibly in a tendency to 'live for today and let tomorrow take care of itself', but it is also present in the confidence needed to establish the unemployment centres, credit unions, and housing co-operatives which have sprung up in the working class districts of Merseyside in recent years. The estates have also seen improvements in crime rates, school attendance and voting turnout, and some residents are expressing their commitment to these areas by purchasing their council houses. However, this picture of responses to unemployment also includes more ambivalent elements, such as the practice of young people working away from Liverpool, leaving Sunday nights, living in shared flats in the South during the week, and returning on Fridays.

6.14 In Scotland the ICRP selected Glasgow and the Clydeside conurbation, and SCEL have studies underway on Aberdeen and Kirkaldy, but CURS is not represented in Scotland. Two particular themes emerge from this research. One is an interest in the social impact of oil developments in Aberdeen and elsewhere in Scotland, and the second is a concern, still remarkably absent south of the border, to understand the relationship between social mobility and migration. In contrast, Wales and Northern Ireland are poorly represented in locality research (but see reference to Harris below).

6.15 Southern England does figure in locality research, but in a strangely uneven manner. The South West region is particularly well endowed with the ICRP study of Bristol, the SCEL work on Swindon and the CURS research on Swindon and Cheltenham. In contrast, East Anglia is not represented at all in the locality research efforts of the main programmes, which is surprising since this region contains many of the free-standing towns which have experienced rapid job growth in the recent period. The South East has attracted far less attention than its size and complexity demands. And once again, despite the dynamism of the regional economy, much of the research effort has been directed towards areas of declining job opportunities. The major loss of manufacturing jobs was the principal theme in the ICRP study of London, and the CURS locality in the South East is Thanet, which is very much on the wrong side of the 'South/South divide'. The exception is the interesting work being carried out on the south Hampshire area by Mason and others at Southampton University.

6(iii) Impacts of employment change on household relations; the experience of unemployment

6.1 The locality studies discussed in the previous Section vary enormously in style and perspective, but they are all concerned with how people have experienced economic restructuring. In this Section we review literature which, for the most part, is not cast in a 'locality study' mould, but which is nevertheless very relevant to an understanding of urban change in Britain today. The main theme is the way in which employment change, and especially unemployment, is experienced either by the individuals involved or by members of households containing such individuals.

6.17 Several of the classic studies in the twentieth century development of the social sciences investigated the social psychological effects of unemployment on working class men. This history is interestingly treated in the collection edited by **Fryer and Ullah** (1987), in which comparisons are made between the findings of Jahoda in her 1930s research in Marienthal, Austria and in the South Wales coalfield, and the situation in British cities today. Jahoda had found that psychological stress was associated with the loss of access, consequent upon being made unemployed, to certain categories of experience. These categories of experience were:

(i) social contact with workmates;

(ii) activity and purposefulness;

(iii) a feeling that one is making a positive contribution to society at large;

(iv) status and respect; and

(v) a routine daily timetable.

The relevance of these categories to the 1980s is confirmed in several of the papers in this book and, in the study on Brighton, it is shown that unemployed women feel the loss of access to four out of five of these categories of experience just as keenly as unemployed men.

6.18 The study on 'Redundancy and Recession in South Wales' by Harris et al from the Unemployment Research Group at Swansea is particularly important in this context. Among the many interesting findings are Tables which show the many kinds of employment and unemployment experiences that people have had since redundancy. A sizeable proportion (21%) had

'chequered' work histories in which spells of employment were mixed with unemployment, self-employment and retraining. This greatly effects the impact of redundancy, not only on the individual concerned but on their families as well. Harris et al suggest that this group is now so important that it might be regarded as a new underprivileged class fraction in British society.

6.19 Most of the research which is concerned with the impact of recession takes a close look at changing household structures and relations. In some cases the interest is highly specific, for example, to find out if the social security system encourages the wives of unemployed men to withdraw from paid work, but more often the interest is to discover the way in which 'households' cope with unemployment, poor job prospects and low pay, and the confusingly complicated system of family income support.

6.20 One of the most influential writers on the household in contemporary Britain is **Ray Pahl.** In his earlier work, he suggested that the growing use of female labour and the unemployment of large numbers of men would lead to a reversal of household relationships with men taking over more of the housekeeping roles while women became the main links of households to the formal economy. The informal economy would also emerge as an alternative to labour-contract paid work, and people would compensate for unemployment by moving into the black economy. These views were echoed by Urry, who argued that de-industrialisation would enhance the salience of households in social life. Subsequent research, however, has demonstrated that this view is largely mistaken. One of the most vocal critics has been Lydia Morris (see below), but Pahl's own later work serves to modify the picture he presented in his influential 1980 paper. In 'Divisions of Labour' (Pahl 1984) he reports on a survey of 700 households on the Isle of Sheppey in Kent which traces the effects of economic decline on the informal economy and on household relations. He found that there was little evidence of a buoyant informal economy. In particular, households with unemployed men lacked the resources necessary to purchase the tools and materials needed for informal work, and isolation from workplace contacts further reduced opportunities in this respect. Furthermore, households with unemployed members could not engage as effectively in 'self-provisioning' such as DIY. This difference led Pahl to argue that there was growing polarisation of households taking place, those with members in work could augment their income in various ways, whilst those with unemployment not only lacked the income from that employment, but the advantages from work in the informal and domestic spheres which that income could generate.

6.21 The tendency within this important literature on household responses to urban economic change has been to present the household as a harmonious unit. This has been criticised by those interested in gender relations in households experiencing male unemployment. Perhaps the most influential research on this topic has been conducted by **Lydia Morris** (1987). She carried out surveys in Port Talbot, South Wales (where her research was part of the work discussed under Harris 1987 above) and in Hartlepool. In Port Talbot household interviews were conducted eighteen months after large scale redundancies in the local steelworks. Domestic circumstances were greatly affected by male unemployment, but not always in ways that one might expect. For example, with the man at home the domestic duties of the woman generally went up rather than down. And, with declining job opportunities for women, gender role reversal in the domestic sphere was virtually unknown. Furthermore, traditional gender ideology remained a strong force, and a move towards a man carrying out 'women's work' was resisted by both partners. Men often slightly increased their contributions to domestic labour (at least in the early stages of unemployment) but not enough to challenge the woman's control (including financial control) of the routine aspects of the domestic economy. Renegotiation of the domestic division of labour was particularly unlikely when the men retained their membership of an all-male social group. The exception to this rule was when the man did major alterations to the house; but this, after all, was no threat to traditional gender roles. In fact, home alterations constituted one of the main uses to which redundancy monies were put.

6.22 Morris' work stands in an uneasy relationship to other research on urban change. She criticises CURS for not being properly equipped anthropologically or sociologically to conduct research on the household, and she is doubtful about the use of local labour markets as a central theme in both CURS and SCEL. But she is also critical of Pahl's work, which she sees as being too much of a 'snap-shot', too unconcerned with the organisation of, or responsibility for, household finances, too prepared to see the household as a cohesive unit, and not sufficiently concerned to explain the variations between households. But, with Pahl, she agrees that it is important to bring together the economic and the domestic, and to treat unpaid work as a serious category.

Evaluation

6.23 Or evaluation of the research discussed in this Chapter is as follows:

(i) our understanding of the relationships between economic restructuring and social change as they are played out in specific localities is likely to be dramatically improved as a result of the CURS and SCEL initiatives;

(ii) many strands of research came together to form the sudden popularity of Locality Studies in the 1980s. These are shown diagrammatically in Figure 3. Two features of this diagram are particularly noteworthy: the first is the significance of developments classified under the political economy perspective, and the second is the number of social science disciplines which became involved in Locality Research during this period;

(iii) we accept that broad economic changes lead to a restructuring of production. However, different firms, even within the same sector, will choose different restructuring strategies, resulting in a great variety of local effects, and so it is impossible to read off labour market changes, local class structures and local politics from a knowledge of the economic base of an area; and

(iv) it is clear that the current emphasis on the significance of the household is fully justified, but we feel that the category 'household' must be critically examined, and that insufficient research has been conducted on the nature of, and spatial variations in, relationships within the household.

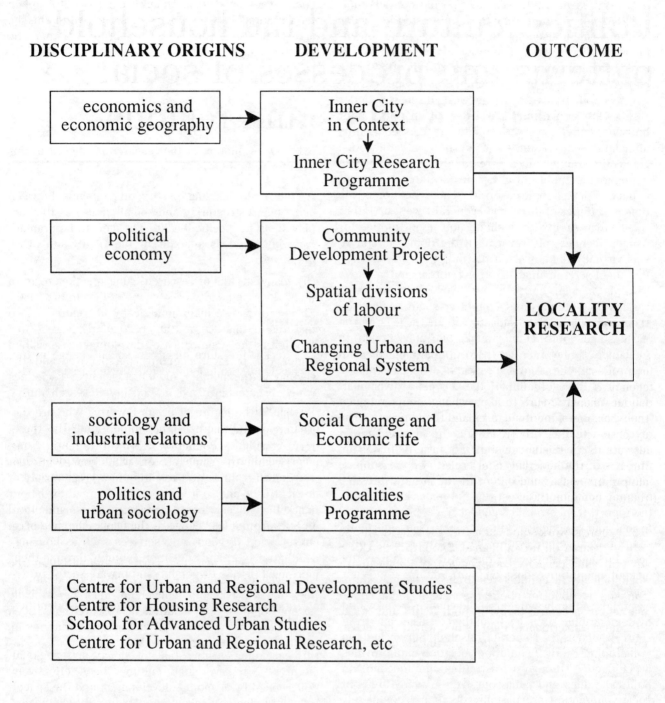

| DISCIPLINARY ORIGINS | DEVELOPMENT | OUTCOME |

Figure 3 : The Antecedents of Locality Research

CHAPTER 7

Politics, culture and the household: patterns and processes of social change in UK cities and regions

Introduction

7.1 It is widely accepted that important changes in urban lifestyles, values and forms of association have taken place in the recent period. But precisely what is it that has changed? How have the changes come about? And what have been the causes and the consequences of these changes? There are two reasons why the answers to these questions are not easy to find. The first lies in the generality and breadth of the subject matter of social change. Because of this the present Chapter contains the most diverse material of any in the report. It incorporates gender, race, politics (both formal and practical), culture, social class and consumption, together with the many relationships between them. The second reason for difficulty is the lack of quantitative data on many of the important aspects of social and cultural change. The bare essentials of family and household change are provided by demographic statistics from the censuses, and from sources such as the General Household Survey and the Longitudinal Study. In addition, electoral data provides a perspective (though a frustratingly limited one) on political values and behaviour. Yet so many areas of social interaction are partially or almost completely hidden from view, usually because they are strenuously defended as private and personal (moral attitudes, relationships within the home, behaviour towards non-conforming minorities, etc).

7.2 These problems have not, however, deflected attention away from changes in urban lifestyles, values and forms of association. This is because it was increasingly realised that these changes were not just reflective of other developments, such as those in the spheres of work and employment, and in the physical contexts of our lives, but that they also contained the power to shape such changes.

Issues

7.3 Recent literature on urban social change in the UK has tended to focus on the following issues:

(i) what is the nature of urban poverty? Who are the urban poor and where are they to be found? Has there been a tendency for social groups to become more polarised than previously? And if so, how does this show itself in the patterns of urban social change?

(ii) is there a new social geography of consumption emerging in the UK? How are changes in the modes of consumption of goods and services such as housing, health, transport and education (notably through their increasing private ownership and private sector provision), affecting our cities? Are they serving to alter attitudes and lifestyles so as to change class identities and voting behaviour?

(iii) can one sensibly talk of 'local and regional cultures'? Or have such cultures been effectively undermined by economic development and the space-reducing effects of telecommunications? Specifically, are there significant urban and regional differences in political values, and race and gender relations, beyond those accounted for by differences in social class and levels of consumption?

(iv) what has been the geography of social unrest, as manifested in inner city riots and major industrial conflicts? And how is this geography to be explained? How do age, class and race intersect to produce particular patterns of connection and exclusion? Can it be said that British cities are witnessing the emergence of 'antagonistic spaces'? And

(v) what do all these changes imply for the distribution of power? And how has the distribution of power been affected by changing local-central relations? Why have certain local governments developed radical interventionist policies? And why has popular and research interest in local government increased at a time when its powers are being taken away from it?

Contributions

7(i) General studies of social change in the UK

7.4   Much of the literature on social, cultural and political change in the UK over the last twenty years takes a broad national perspective and is not primarily concerned with how these changes vary from one city to another, or between the inner city and the rest. However, urban research has often drawn upon this broader literature, not only for information about general trends, but also for ideas about the processes which lie behind the recorded spatial changes.

7.5   The kind of research which has a considerable relevance to urban change is that which results from a renewed interest in the life cycle or lifecourse. A recent collection of papers on this theme (Bryman et al. [eds] 1987) contains several such studies. **Angela Dale's** Chapter, for example, examines the connections between stage in the life cycle and key social variables such as:

(i) access to paid employment;

(ii) net disposable income; and

(iii) ownership of certain significant assets such as a house, car, central heating, freezer, etc.

Using data from the General Household Survey for 1979, she shows that these connections vary markedly between households in different life cycle stages. The three commonest household types, for example, show contrasting profiles. Couples with one or more dependent children tend to score very high on assets, low on income and high on hours in paid work. Older working-age couples without children at home score high on all three bases, while elderly single-person households score very low on all three bases. The relevance of these connections to an understanding of urban social change becomes clear when it is realised how selective, with respect to life cycle stage, the suburbanisation process of the post-war period has been. In general, the couples with children are to be found in the inner suburbs and on the outer council estates, older working couples without children in the outer private estates, and the single elderly either in the inner city or outside the city altogether.

7.6   Another type of general study which affects our understanding of urban change focuses on the controversial issues surrounding social class in modern Britain. The key work here is **Goldthorpe** et al's 'Social Mobility and Class Structure in Modern Britain' first published in 1980, but updated in a revised edition in 1987. Their study shows that despite measures designed to create a more open society, that is, one in which the barriers to social mobility would be lowered through improvements in education etc., the British class structure has retained a remarkable resistance to change, and striking inequalities of life chances, related to the circumstances of one's birth, remain. During the long post-war boom this did not matter too much because the upward movement into the service class was not accompanied by a worsening of the positions of those in manual working class occupations. Since the late 1970s, however, this is no longer the case, and many of those with manual working class backgrounds have experienced downward mobility into unemployment. Goldthorpe et al then emphasise that far and away the most important change in the British class structure during the recent period has been the rapid growth of the service class (professional, technical and managerial workers). At the same time there has been a decline in male manual work and an increase in unemployment so that by the early 1980s the proportion of all men of working class origins who were themselves employed in manual wage-earning jobs had fallen to about 40%. This decline, they claim, goes a long way towards explaining the poor performance of the Labour Party in recent general elections, and for this reason they distance themselves from the 'class de-alignment thesis' of political change in Britain (see below).

7.7   In this matter Goldthorpe's research stands in an interesting relationship to that of **Marshall** et al. (1988), who compare Goldthorpe's analysis with that based upon the influential conceptual scheme developed by the American Marxist, Eric Ohlin Wright. This latter research focuses attention on the level of autonomy that employees have in the workplace (related to their managerial skills or educational qualifications), which serve to differentiate a privileged middle class from a non-privileged working class. Marshall et al. show that, in general, the Goldthorpe scheme is superior to that of Wright when it comes to analysing social class in contemporary Britain.

7(ii) The geography of social change: urban and regional social demography; local class structures; social segregation

7.8   The 1980s have witnessed a resurgence of interest in relations between the social and the spatial. In a previous generation this relationship was researched through 'community studies'. These had the advantage that they placed social relations in a specific locational context, and confronted the complex ecological or 'within-place' interdependencies between material environment, economy and culture. However, despite the emphasis in several of these studies on social change brought about by influences external to the community, these works were generally poorly suited to the task of revealing the spatial or 'between-place' interdependencies. Such connections increasingly linked the lives of people living at considerable distances from one another.

7.9 The concern for the social and the spatial in the 1980s has largely focused on the relationships between social class and locality, and also on the role and significance of local social networks. Places (regions, cities, neighbourhoods) are seen as having been socially produced and to possess characteristics which are largely determined by their local class configurations. At the same time, both local and national class structures and relations are shaped by geography. In specific historical and social contexts geography facilitates or deters, permits or excludes, those kinds of behaviours (such as collective action to oppose exploitation) which serve to determine social outcomes.

7.10 By far the commonest type of empirical research on the intersection of the social and the spatial takes the form of studies of social segregation. These examine either the spatial distribution of social classes or the spatial distribution of racial minorities. Specifically, they show that the working class tend to be located in the inner city and on peripheral council estates, and the middle class in the suburbs, while 'Afro-Caribbeans' and 'Asians' concentrate in the inner city. Religious segregation does not attracted much research attention, despite the fact that it was the basis of segregation in the recent pasts of several large British cities. Today, it is the dominant feature in just one of them — Belfast. And **Freddy Boal** has made this city the focus of much of his research in social geography.

7.11 In his work on spatial segregation in Belfast published in 1982 he argues that the Protestant and Catholic communities are ethnic groups, and that Northern Ireland society is both culturally and institutionally pluralist. Following research conducted in the United States, he asserts that spatial (residential) segregation is inversely related to degree of assimilation (i.e. the greater the spatial separation of ethnic groups, the lower their social integration). He adds that once residential segregation exists, it can help to reinforce division between the groups, thus making assimilation more difficult to achieve. At the same time residential segregation assists social and cultural integration within the group. This is because it reduces outside contacts which might otherwise serve to dilute the group's distinctive character. The rest of his paper consists of a discussion of these ideas in relation to the evolving patterns of residential segregation in Belfast during the twentieth century.

7.12 Twentieth century ethnic segregation in Belfast has its origins in the movement of rural Catholics to the city during the phase of rapid urbanisation in the mid- and late nineteenth century. His data shows clearly that in the period 1911 to 1972, the degree of street-level segregation increased significantly, so that by the latter date 78% of Protestants lived on streets which had less than 10% Catholics (and 60% of Catholics lived on streets where there were less than 10% Protestants). What is more, a large part of that increase in segregation had occurred in the years 1969–72, that is, since the start of 'The Troubles'. Boal recognises that Belfast had expanded beyond its city boundaries and that, to the extent that the outer suburbs were less segregated, the figures might overstate the degree of division between the groups. But he concludes this section of the paper by saying that it seems very unlikely that assimilation had increased over this time.

7.13 He then focuses attention on the areas where ethnic mixing was occurring to find out what kinds of people lived there. Two such areas were identified, one running north from the city centre along the Antrim Road, and the other just to the south/southeast of the centre. He discovers that those who lived in larger owner occupied housing, both Catholic and Protestant were the least segregated, while those who lived in public sector housing (especially Catholics) were the most segregated. When it came to perceptions of change, the areas which were less than 30% Catholic were thought to be becoming more Protestant, and those which were more than 30% Catholic were thought (especially by Protestants) to be becoming more Catholic. Information on date of movement into the residence confirms this picture of Protestant retreat in areas with more than 30% Catholics. The Catholics in these areas were largely newcomers to the district. Boal suggests that resistance to the arrival of Catholics was weakened by the fact that many of the Protestants were moving out to the new council estates built on the outskirts of the city predominantly for them. They were choosing to 'exit' rather than 'voice' their discontent. He concludes, therefore, that especially in working class areas, much of the ethnic mixing is transitional in nature.

7.14 Finally Boal inteprets the higher degree of segregation of working class households as reflecting: (i) their stronger local social networks which tie them into their area of residence much more than middle class households. For working class households 'the neighbourhood is an extension of the house'; (ii) the competition for houses and jobs among working class households; and (iii) the fear shared by Protestants of what might happen if Catholics were allowed to live in a Protestant street — that is, that this number would increase rapidly to become a majority.

7(iii) The social geography of consumption

7.15   One of the most significant conceptual shifts in urban and regional studies in the recent period has been the 'rediscovery' of consumption, after a time when the whole weight of theoretical inquiry and empirical research had been placed upon production. In part, this shift came about through the persistence of those who drew inspiration from the Weberian branch of political economy at a time when writers from the Marxist branch were at their most influential. But it also came from Marxist forms of analysis via the notion of 'collective consumption' developed by the French school of urban sociology and expressed most powerfully in the work of Manuel Castells.

7.16   Perhaps because of this, the emphasis in studies of the urban dimension of consumption have tended to focus heavily on the consumption of services provided totally or to a significant extent by the public sector (such as health, education, transport, housing and social security). For example, the geography of the national health service, and of the growing private health sector has attracted particular attention. The main theme of the literature is that there is a growing divide between those who are well off and those who are poor in their access to health care, and that this is leading to a widening of social class and spatial differences in mortality and morbidity.

7.17   An example of this research is provided by **Curtis and Mohan** in their study of north-south differences in ill-health and health care. They begin by demonstrating that a distinctive north-south divide exists in the health of the population. Standardised Mortality Rates (SMRs) were between 5 and 11% above the England and Wales figure for the Northern, North West, Yorkshire and Humberside and West Midlands regions, and between 6 and 9% below the average in East Anglia, South West and South East regions. What is more, these north-south differences persist if one standardises for type of area. In other words the north does not do worse because the SMRs are higher in urban areas than in rural ones. The authors then turn to the differences in health revealed by the Health and Lifestyle Survey in 1985. This shows that self-reported ill-health was also more common in the north. The same pattern emerged from the estimates produced by the Royal College of Physicians of death-rates due to disease induced by smoking. Finally, the Regional Heart Study revealed major differences between northern towns and southern ones, and these differences were only partially accounted for by variations in social class, climate and water hardness.

7.18   Curtis and Mohan then turn to the health services. They point out that the regional inequalities inherited by the NHS were virtually frozen by incremental budgeting and fifteen years of minimal capital investment so that London and the South East remained for a long time better served by hospital services than other parts of the country. To counteract this, following the Resource Allocation Working Party report in 1976, resources were deliberately redirected to favour the under-funded regions. The gap has indeed narrowed in the period since the mid-1970s, but in the recent period, with no growth in resources overall, their reallocation has implied a painful reduction in the funds available to District Health Authorities in the south, notably in London.

7.19   A further aspect of the north-south divide in health provision is the problem of recruitment of staff, particularly in London. As a low wage employer in a high cost region, the NHS cannot compete with other sectors, or indeed with the private sector of the health service. This has led to a heavy use of agency staff. Curtis and Mohan then examine the private sector to show that 23% of the service class are covered by private health insurance (mostly paid for as a bonus by the employer), whereas only 2% of semi- and unskilled manual workers are covered. This is reflected in a strong bias towards the South East in levels of private health insurance, with rates in the Northern, Yorkshire and Humberside, Wales and North West regions being less than 50% those in the South East outside Greater London. As the authors say, 'there is an emerging spatial division of welfare: overlying the State's attempt to equalise service availability is a new pattern of inequality in access to facilities'.

7(iv) Changing local and regional cultures; place and politics

7.20   In recent years there has been an active debate about the significance of local and regional cultures in Britain. Some writers emphasise the local and regional cultural differences which are revealed through the everyday lives of ordinary people (practical cultures). Such differences are thought to be decreasing for two reasons: firstly, as a result of the powerful standardising influences of mass popular culture, especially as communicated through television programmes and advertising. Secondly, as a result of the growth of more privatised and home-based life styles, which implies that people have less contact with others in the local area. Other writers, however, emphasise the cultural differences which are revealed in the strong feelings that people express about the people, things and places which form the context to their lives (symbolic cultures). Far from diminishing there are signs that these identifications are as keenly felt today as they ever were in the past. We are said to become aware of our local culture only in opposition to other 'outside' cultures. This implies that the very same connections which might serve to undermine differences in practical cultures, could at the same time enhance the awareness of symbolic cultural differences (such as those which distinguish 'white' neighbourhoods from 'black', inner city from suburb, etc).

7.21 These practical and symbolic cultures can have considerable importance for urban change in contemporary Britain. Planning conflicts often reflect struggles over the identity of places (country village v. dormitory suburb, market town v. industrial city). Local culture can be used as a local 'resource' to be drawn upon to achieve purposeful collective action (see reference to pro-activity in 6.9). On the other hand, conflicts between cultures can lead to disinvestment (as has happened in areas affected by the riots of 1981 and 1985, and in Northern Ireland since 1969). Perhaps the main significance of these cultural differences lies in the way they affect social and political relationships in the inner city. At the centre of the idea of culture is the notion that people share different 'maps of meaning' (**Jackson** 1989); this implies that it is extraordinarily difficult for a person brought up in one culture to understand and sympathise with the 'taken-for-granted worlds' of those brought up in an other. The possibilities for misunderstanding are legion, and stereotyping abounds.

7.22 This is where ethnographic research, drawing upon the methods of anthropology, might be able to help. There are few good examples of this perspective applied to British cities. Perhaps the best known is **Sandra Wallman's** (1984) study of eight households in Battersea, south London. Wallman begins by describing the way that our image of the inner city has been shaped by the close association that we make (helped by the media) between three elements: disadvantage, the inner city as a place, and minority ethnic status. Hence, she says, the popular idea that ethnic minorities (who happen to live in the inner city) are disadvantaged, and that inner city areas (which happen to house sizeable minority group populations) are unpleasant places to live in. 'As the ways we classify people and places both reflect and confirm these assumptions, the terms we use and the ways we use them do not simply affect our understanding of events, they may also influence those events, even to the extent of moving them in directions which no one intended'. In other words the language we use to describe the inner city is not neutral; it can actually serve to stigmatise the inner city and the people who live there.

7.23 Wallman then refutes our expectations in two ways. She claims that her research shows that race is not central or even consistently important in the daily lives of her residents, and that the inner city is not a bleak tale of deprivation and disadvantage. To develop these points further she lists the 'capabilities of the inner city environment', and the resources available to its inhabitants. These resources are extended beyond material things to include 'time', 'information' and 'identity'. Much of the remainder of the book consists of detailed studies of eight households. From these she draws certain conclusions: firstly, that the variety of situations found in the inner city is very great; secondly, that the options offered by the inner city — its 'capabilities' — are many. With such a wide range of industries making up the local economy, and with the possibility of access to jobs elsewhere through the dense transport network, the inner city can be said to have 'resilience' to recession. Thirdly, that if people do not use local support it is because they do not need to. They still identify with the area, recognise one another, and do not feel alienated by their urban situation. And finally, that all eight households were viable in the sense that they knew about resources, obtained access to them, and managed them appropriately.

7.24 The significance of ethnographic research lies not so much in what it has already achieved but in what it promises for the future. It offers the possibility that analyses of the inner city might penetrate beyond the macro-categories such as 'race', gender and class to address the complexities of the situations which inner city residents face. In the absence of such an understanding it is unlikely that we will be able to explain or predict the way that those who live in the inner city will respond to external economic or political changes.

7(v) Race and ethnicity, minority and youth cultures; social control and popular unrest — riots; the ecology of crime

7.25 There is a large and wide-ranging literature on these topics. Much of the research in the 1960s and 1970s followed the lead taken by Rex and Moore in their study of Sparkbrook, Birmingham ('Race, Community and Conflict') in which they identified the connections between race, housing tenure and location, and showed how those of Asian and Afro-Caribbean descent lost out in the competition for decent housing. Since then, the focus has turned towards the nature and incidence of white racism, the continuation, despite equal opportunities legislation, of forms of social closure which work against black people, and the role that 'race' plays in British politics. The 1980s, however, have seen a major new focus for research. There has been a lively debate about 'the roots of urban unrest', following the urban riots in 1981 and 1985 in many British cities.

7.26 In their collection of essays entitled 'The Roots of Urban Unrest', **Benyon and Solomos**, bring together a variety of authors. While most are academics and community workers, they also include a Deputy Assistant Commissioner of the Metropolitan Police, and Lord Scarman, the author of the Report on the Brixton Riots of 1981. Popular explanations of the riots, such as those which claim that they were simply acts of base criminality, or that they were fomented and orchestrated by foreign-trained revolutionaries, are roundly dismissed. The editors claim that they wish to go beyond the other popular view, that the riots were caused by social deprivation, racial discrimination and unemployment. But it is clear that most of the contributions seek the causes of the riots in this area. However, the emphasis varies; Benyon points out that while the 'trigger events' in each case involved police officers and black people, the areas in which the riots occurred shared five significant characteristics: they were areas of racial disadvantage and discrimination; they all had high unemployment levels especially for young people and especially for young blacks; deprivation was widespread in that the areas had poor environments, bad housing, poor social facilities and high crime rates; the people in those areas experienced political exclusion and powerlessness; and finally, mistrust of, and hostility towards, the police was widespread in each of these areas. Stuart Hall uses rather different language. He emphasises the alienation of the black population from mainstream society and the way in which this has been exacerbated by the political and economic changes since 1979. He writes (p47):

> 'When public policies are ... redirected so as to enable the combination of possessive individualism, a strong and disciplinary state and the wild and untutored forces of the free market to prevail, it is slightly obscene to ask the question why those who are on the receiving end of those processes sometimes get so angry that they throw a brick!'

He also emphasises racism, particularly as it is experienced through the relationships that black people have with the main institutions in our society.

7.27 Several contributors then stress the significance of the very poor relations between black people and the police. Richard Wells, the police officer in charge of Northwest London at the time of the Broadwater Farm riot suggests many ways that the policing of inner city areas could be improved, but he also repeats his view that those who participated in the riots gained three things, excitement in place of boredom, profit from looting and a feeling of power in place of 'a sort of helplessness.' This emphasis on helplessness is picked up by John Rex who asserts (p104) that the problem is one of ghettoisation and that 'as long as we of the city, administer them, in the inner city ghetto or colony, there will be lacking that level of mutual respect which is the precondition of social peace.' The editors concluded at the end of the book that there were few

signs that the injustices experienced by black people were being eradicated, or that the participation by blacks in the political process so necessary for consent to develop, was beginning to occur. They therefore share the gloomy prognosis that urban unrest on the scale experienced in 1981 and 1985 will return to Britain's inner cities.

7.28 The previous section dealt only with 'racial' minorities in the inner areas of British cities. There is a small but growing literature on other ethnically distinct groups such as Jews, and those of Irish descent, and of other minorities such as Gypsies. But perhaps the most stimulating research on minority cultures in British cities has been that on youth lifestyles, initiated by the Centre for Contemporary Cultural Studies at the University of Birmingham. This research emphasises the way that young working class kids tend to express their opposition to their 'structural subordination' through their rejection of school and of the middle class values that it represents. This then excludes them from middle class jobs, with the result that their resistance has led them to collude in their own oppression.

7.29 Some minorities in British cities are more than just out of step in their values and lifestyles, they engage in activities which the state, usually with strong popular support, defines as being unlawful. Drug 'abuse' is a case in point; it is widely practised, is socially condoned in certain contexts, (such as the use of marijuana among many Afro-Caribbeans), but it is a crime. Research on crime in the city is increasingly aware of the social construction of criminality, and of the significant extent to which crime statistics are affected by reporting behaviours and policing practices.

7.30 In the opening pages of her book 'Crime, Space and Society' **Susan Smith** shows that she is well aware of these problems in the analysis of the causes and context of crime in the inner cities of Britain. She then turns to official crime statistics and the results of the British Crime Survey, to show that crime rates were higher in urban regions than in rural ones, and that they were particularly high in the inner cities. Here all types of crime were above the national average, but burglary, theft from persons, robbery and sexual offences were all more than twice the national average. Drawing upon a detailed empirical study of north central Birmingham, she then discusses the high crime rates there in terms of three possibilities:

(i) that they are high because of the high concentration there of the residences of offenders;

(ii) that they reflect the abundance of opportunities for crime in an inner city environment; and

(iii) that they are high because of the characteristics and behaviours of the victims themselves.

Her data shows that there is a high concentration of offenders in her areas, that the offender rate was more than three times higher for the unemployed than for the employed, that many of the offenders were young (one-third of school age) and that many young offenders carried out their criminal activity in a group (indicating shared delinquent values). Housing tenure differences played only a small role, with offenders slightly more likely to come from private-rented accommodation, or council housing than from owner occupation, but those living in apartments were much more likely to offend than those living in houses, and those in areas of housing stress (HAAs) more than those living elsewhere in the inner city. Nearly sixty percent of the employed offenders were from social classes four and five (semi-skilled and unskilled manual workers). Mean distances between residence and location of crime (journey to crime) were low in this inner area averaging just over two miles; this reflects the low mobility of the offenders themselves and links the high crime rates to the presence of offender residences. Susan Smith then proceeds to accept the argument that older inner city housing does tend to offer a 'soft target' for burglary and that the opportunity side of the equation is favourable to high crime rates.

7.31   The next section of the book is concerned with the victim of inner city crime and asks why, and in what ways, are inner city residents vulnerable to crime? It shows that the victims are more likely to be those with particular urban lifestyles, notably ones that involve going out frequently and leaving the house unattended for long periods of time. 'Those most susceptible are not the old and infirm, but the young and mobile. The relatively affluent and the relatively advantaged.' (p.96–7) In particular, it is the areas which have a more affluent appearance in the inner city (such as the GIAs) which seem to be the target for burglary. For violent crime the victims were, in more than a third of the cases, associates of the offenders and the crime grew out of a relationship that went sour; so the sharp distinction between victim and offender is not appropriate in many cases.

7.32   In the last part of the study, Smith discusses the effects of crime and the social reactions to crime. She points out that in her Birmingham inner city area, white residents are more likely than Afro-Caribbeans or Asians to feel unsafe and to be concerned that the crime rate was high and rising. Their fear is fed by the reporting of crimes in the local press, which then combines with rumour and folk wisdom, to produce danger maps of the area, typically drawn along racial boundaries. She then argues that this fear of crime is itself a problem in the inner city and one of the main obstacles to improved race relations in Britain.

7(vi) Voting patterns and processes; party support, class interests and location

7.33   The last two sections have concentrated on social and cultural situations and events in British inner cities. But changes in values and social relations are not confined to the inner city, nor are the interesting contrasts only between the inner city, the suburbs and the 'urbanised countryside'. There are some indications that Britain's cities have become less alike during the recent period, and that, though these differences may be rooted in economic restructuring, they are manifested in changes in political culture which are made visible by the way in which people vote at general elections.

7.34   Recent electoral research in Britain has been dominated by the debate on the class dealignment thesis. This holds that the loyalty of voters to the political party which traditionally represents their interests, has been diminishing, that this leads to volatility in electoral behaviour, and that, in particular, traditional Labour voters have been deserting the Labour Party to vote for the centre parties or for the Conservatives. This suggestion fitted neatly with both the 'end of ideology' theme in social theory, and the supposed 'embourgeoisement' effects of wider home ownership and general improvements in living standards. However, this class dealignment thesis has come under attack from three directions. Firstly, it has been shown that part of the dealignment was more apparent than real, and that the relationship between social class and voting reasserts itself when more detailed occupational categories are used, and when the position of wives (usually ascribed the class status of their husbands) is properly taken into account. Secondly, the decline of the Labour vote can be shown to have resulted in large measure not from the desertion of the unskilled manual workers in manufacturing industry from the Labour Party, but from the sharp decline in the proportion of the population which falls into this 'core' working class group. Finally, it ignores the particularities of Party fortunes and policy stances; arguably the Labour Party reached a low point in 1983, just at the time when the class-dealignment thesis was being developed.

7.35   One variant of the class dealignment thesis has, however, stood up to empirical testing, and has particular relevance to an understanding of urban change in the recent period. This is the 'Miller paradox', which states that while the relationship between class location and voting may be weakening at the individual level, it is becoming more important at the constituency, level. Thus, in areas which are predominantly working class, 'natural' Conservative voters increasingly tend to support Labour, while in areas dominated by the 'middle class', 'natural' Labour voters increasingly tend to vote Conservative.

7.36 Johnston and Pattie test this idea (along with many others) in their spatial analysis of voting patterns in Britain 1975–87 (**Johnston and Pattie** 1989). They show firstly that the allegiance of three key occupational groups (administrative/managerial, professional, and unskilled manual workers) to the Parties which best represent their interests has weakened over this period, with far greater variation in levels of support across constituencies. They then regress votes for Conservative, Labour and Alliance, by these three occupations against seven constituency variables, to show not only that the relationships take the expected form (for example, that the Labour votes of administrators and managers go up in areas of high unemployment), but that the relationships generally become stronger over the 1975–87 period. This means that the 'neighbourhood effect' at the level of the constituency was becoming increasingly important. The next step was to separate out constituency level effects from those of the functional and the geographical regions within which the constituencies were located. The latter levels of aggregation also proved to be significant. Thus for geographical regions they show that in the administrative and managerial occupational class several northern regions — especially the three in Scotland — have percentages voting Conservative up to 20 (%) points lower than that in the outer southeast, but only in Strathclyde, Merseyside and South Yorkshire was there a clear increase in the difference over time. For Labour voting, on the other hand, such a trend was clearly evident in 11 regions, with a major increase in the differences between those regions and the outer southeast between 1979 and 1987. This increased spatial polarisation for the geographical regions was not matched, however, by an increased polarisation for the functional type of place; this means that, while 'Labour type' places, such as 'poor inner city' areas attracted far more Labour votes from administrators and managers than did agricultural areas, the differences did not widen over time.

7.37 These results support both the class dealignment thesis, and the 'Miller' explanation of it, which emphasises the growing importance of the spatial context in influencing voting behaviour. The significance of this for urban change, is that a spatial polarisation of political cultures, with Labour becoming stronger in its strongholds and the Conservatives in theirs, might imply that 'new right' types of urban regeneration policy will be increasingly resisted in precisely those areas where the need for regeneration is greatest, that is, in the larger conurbations of northern and western Britain.

7(vii) Changing central-local relations; local government

7.38 The salience of urban and regional changes in political values would have been far greater had it not been for the sharp decrease in the power and influence of local government in the recent period. Even before the changes initiated by the Conservative government after 1979, there had been an active debate about the political significance of local government in Britain, with many writers concerned to demonstrate how little discretion local authorities had in matters affecting the character and pace of urban development. Thus Lord Redcliffe-Maud writing in 1974 on the limits to local government set by the central state, concludes that 'Local authorities are obliged to provide certain services and allowed to provide others. They can do practically nothing else which costs money.' (quoted in Cockburn, C. The Local State, p46).

7.39 Since 1979 the constraints upon local government have become much greater. They have seen their influence on urban housing reduced by the virtual cessation of council house building, by the sale of existing council houses, and, now, by the privatisation of whole council estates. Their role in local education has been reduced by changes in the management of schools which place more power in the hands of parents and local businessmen, and by the 'assisted places' and 'opting out' policies which take children and schools out of the charge of the local education authority. Their influence on the physical development of their districts has been diminished by the frequency with which local authority rejections of planning proposals have been overturned at appeal, and by the avoidance of local authority planning control in special areas such as those which are managed by Urban Development Corporations. Above all, local authority initiative has been constrained by strict and punitive financial control (the most obvious example is 'rate capping'), and by the abolition of metropolitan authorities. This last step is particularly significant; it meant that major British cities are unique in Western Europe (perhaps in the World) in having no city-wide governing bodies or elected councils.

7.40 Given the erosion of local authority functions, it might seem surprising that local politics has figured so prominently in academic research (and in political debate) in the 1980s. In large part this continued interest is due to the fact that conflict between central and local government has been a prominent feature of British politics for most of the last decade. Undoubtedly, it is the central government's attempts at controlling and reducing local authorities' expenditure in Britain which has provided both the major political and academic focus of interest over recent years. However, there are other reasons. Firstly, the fact that local authorities have become more actively involved in local economic development matters, in the face of a deep manufacturing recession, has permitted research into the roles they are playing. Some authorities, opposed to the Conservative government, have been concerned to demonstrate the potential for alternative social and economic policies by instituting such policies at the local level (the economic effects of the attempt to achieve 'local socialism' are discussed in Section 9(iv) below). Secondly, research into local government has been stimulated by ideas such as Saunders and Cawson's 'dual-state' thesis. This claims that, while central government politics is corporatist, class-based, and largely concerned with matters of economic management for improved production through enhanced competitive advantage, the local authority areas (counties and districts) are the stage for a more pluralist politics concerned primarily with matters of consumption (housing, shopping, education, transport, environment). If 'consumption sector cleavages' (such as the differences between those who use the private sector for housing, transport, education and health and those who depend on the state to provide these services) are as important for the formation of social structures in contemporary Britain as many would claim, the arena of politics which relates to consumption must, according to this view, be similarly significant.

7.41 Research on central-local relations has been greatly advanced in the recent period by the SSRC/ESRC initiative in this area which has produced useful overviews of the nature of these relationships and the ways in which they have changed in the recent period (see in particular Goldsmith's edited volume entitled 'New Research in Central-Local Relations'). The conceptual framework for such studies has been provided by Robert Rhodes who focuses on the recurrent tension between interdependence of centre and locality on the one hand and authoritative decision-making by central government on the other, drawing out the 'asymmetric' nature of the power-dependency relationship. He identifies three distinct trends in the recent period: bargaining in the pre-1974 period; incorporation in the years 1974–79; and direction in the period since 1979.

7.42 It is the detailed effects of this last trend which **Michael Parkinson** narrates in his study of Liverpool as that city teetered on the brink of financial collapse in the early-mid 1980s. Parkinson begins by rooting the conflict between a left-wing local authority and a Conservative central government in the decline of the local economy. This resulted from the virtual closure of the port and from manufacturing disinvestment. This, in turn, produced very high unemployment, and a heavy dependence, firstly, upon transfer payments (social welfare) and, secondly, upon public sector employment. When cuts in public expenditure were brought in by the Conservative government, they threatened both of these fragile bases of the Liverpool economy.

7.43 Deteriorating economic conditions helped to produce an environment suited to violent social protest

(the Toxteth riots of 1981), and to the development of an extreme form of oppositional politics (that of the Militant Tendency). The Labour Party had been less powerful in Liverpool than in other industrial cities, due to sectarian divisions in the working class, brought about by Irish immigration. This allowed the Liberals to form minority administrations for six out of the eight years between 1974 and 1982. The Liberals placed a low priority on council housing and attempted to keep council spending to a low level. The combination of 'political incoherence' and poor service provision which resulted from this period provided a basis for the rise of the younger Labour Party activists. Usually these were members of the Militant Tendency, and many of them came from the public sector unions (especially NALGO and the GMB). The scene was set for an outright confrontation between a militant left-wing administration in Liverpool and a 'new right' government in London.

7.44 The bulk of Parkinson's study describes in detail the budgetary crises of Liverpool council over the years 1983–5 as it attempted to sustain socialist policies locally in the face of cuts in its income from central government. The socialist nature of the policies was reflected in the council's determination to expand its house building programme and an equal determination to see that there were 'no cuts in jobs and services and no rent and rate rises to compensate for Tory cuts.' Through clever manoeuvring and imaginative accounting the Labour council won several rounds in its fight with the Conservative government. But the end was inevitable; the Militant Tendency were thrown out of the Labour Party, the Liverpool councillors were penalised for their affrontary and the city eventually fell into line along with other rebel cities in competing for government support.

Evaluation

7.45 Our conclusions about this rich and varied literature on social change in UK cities are as follows:

(i) that, while it is true that many recent changes serve to mask the differences between social classes (for example separation of ownership and control, wider share-ownership and high levels of working class home ownership), we endorse the view that social class retains its salience as a determinant of opportunities, interests, values and behaviour, and that a key feature of urban change has been the differential presence and uneven growth of the service class;

(ii) despite this emphasis on class we do not deny the importance of consumption sector cleavages in determining local political and economic outcomes. However, despite the current emphasis to the contrary, the division between the public and private sectors is probably as significant in the sphere of production as in that of consumption (for example, the key role of public sector unionisation in shaping support for left-wing policies). Housing tenure plays an important role in shaping political behaviour at certain times and in certain places, but this is a far cry from claiming that consumption has replaced class as the basis for voting;

(iii) nor do we deny the fact that there are other major bases for the formation of social structures in British cities, notably gender, age, and 'race'. Gender relations have been studied intensively in the workplace, but relations outside the workplace remain relatively unexplored. There is a welcome re-emergence of research interest in the 'life-cycle', and research on 'race'

relations in British cities is rightly turning towards the social construction and use of 'racial' categories; and

(iv) we also welcome the entry of a more anthropological style of research on urban change in Britain. Ethnographic research can reveal the 'plurality of cultures' which coexist in British cities and regions, and which help to explain differences in response to national economic and political events. We need to know a lot more about community level social and cultural relationships if we are to explain such notable socio-political trends as the propensity for periodic outbursts of 'popular violence' in inner cities, the emergence of confrontational politics in northern and western Britain, or the spatial polarisation of party support.

CHAPTER 8

The influence of social change, politics and policy on urban built form

8.1 Cities as physical entities act as mirrors to the societies which produce them, one can 'read' them socially and culturally. So much is obvious. But the processes which link built form and land uses to social structure and social relations are far from obvious. This is partly because of inequalities in wealth and power. It is not people in general who shape the city in their own image, but powerful individuals and groups, who, working within and through social and political institutions, influence the structure of the city and the manner and direction of its development. But the complexity of the process arises also from the fact that urban built form and land uses are relatively permanent. This allows disjunctures to develop between the physical form of the city and the social purposes to which that built form is put. Thus change in built form and land use is characteristically 'lumpy' in nature, with long periods of stasis followed by short bursts of rapid development or redevelopment.

Issues

8.2 So in what ways do the towns and cities of the United Kingdom today reflect the changes in politics, culture and social life which have occurred in this country over the last 20 years or so? This broad question can be broken down into a number of researchable issues:

(i) how has the changing class structure impacted on urban built form and spatial structure? More specifically, what has been the effect on the urban landscape of the growth of the service class? Most commentators would turn to the concept of 'gentrification' to help answer these questions. Gentrification has greatly altered the character of many inner city areas in Britain, but it has also been a major feature of social

and physical change in rural areas, especially those located within the commuting range of a large city or possessing special landscape qualities (see Newby's 'Green and Pleasant Land?'). Is gentrification an uncontested process, or are there struggles over the social content and meaning of built form? If there are, how are these struggles manifested, and who are the winners and losers in the process? And

(ii) how have the built forms of British cities been affected by public policies, notably through land use planning and housing policies? Has retreat from the post-war planning system towards a 'freeing up' of development produced any detectable effects on British urban landscapes? To what extent have cities been 'contained' by the operation of green belt policies? How successful has planning been in improving the environments of inner city areas? What impact has the New Towns policy had on the structure of the UK urban system?

8.3 These issues have provoked a lively research literature. This will be reviewed under three headings:

(i) the transformation of parts of the inner city through gentrification;

(ii) the effects of town and country planning, new towns policies etc. on urban land use and built form; and

(iii) the role of housing policies in shaping urban structures.

Contributions

8(i) **The transformation of the inner city through gentrification; rural gentrification**

8.4 The term 'gentrification' is usually used to denote

a process of inner city neighbourhood social change which results in the replacement of a long-established manual working class population, often in privately-rented accommodation, by a career-oriented non-manual middle class population of owner occupiers. Typically, this process is accompanied by investment in housing improvement, sometimes just to bring the housing up to 'modern' standards (for example, through the modernisation of kitchens and bathrooms), but often in order to change the housing structurally (for example, through the alteration of internal layout by knocking down walls between ground floor rooms). It is also sometimes associated with physical improvements to the area through tree-planting, the blocking of roads to prevent through traffic and so on. These social and physical changes then affect local businesses. Old general stores serving working class customers close down, while new shops, restaurants etc. open to meet the more expensive tastes and more specialised needs of the middle class newcomers.

8.5 Research on gentrification carried out in the 1970s identified the main features of the process. We know a great deal about where gentrification occurs (in the older, accessible working class districts in the largest cities, notably London), who the gentrifiers are (young upwardly-mobile professional people), and what kinds of occupational and housing tenure changes accompany gentrification (white-collar employees replace blue-collar, and owner occupation replaces privately-rented accommodation). Since then, research has focussed on two main themes. The first theme concerns the causes of gentrification. Some follow Neil Smith in emphasising the importance of the 'rent gap', that is, the marked difference which sometimes occurs in inner city areas between the value of land and property in its present industrial or working class residential use, and what that land and property would be worth if it were occupied by people or businesses possessing a high social status. Others stress the importance of the growth of the 'service class' and the location at the city centre of many of the private sector jobs (such as those in financial and business services, advertising, the media etc) which members of the service class carry out. Finally there are many who feel uneasy with both of these explanations, and argue instead that the gentrification process should be 'unpacked' to reveal its separate elements. One would then find that many of those who were investing in housing improvement in the inner city are not wealthy now, or likely to be so in the future. Rather, they consist of those who, because of their household situation, cannot afford, or do not need, suburban housing. Included in this category would be career-oriented women without family commitments, the smaller households created by divorce and separation, and dual-career households whose members wish to minimise domestic responsibilities.

8.6 The second recent theme in this literature links gentrification to cultural change. The inner city, or at least parts of it (such as areas of waterfront revitalisation), are regarded as the physical expression of a postmodern society. Unlike the ordered landscapes of the modern period — the suburb in both its private semi-detached, and high-rise council estate forms — the 'postmodern' landscape is that of the inner city. This is not the inner city of row upon row of terrace houses inhabited by the industrial working class, but the inner city which has come into being over the last 15–20 years — culturally pluralist, architecturally varied, a disorganised mixture of lifestyles and environments. The issue here is whether or not these changes in urban land use and built form can be seen as a physical expression of a 'postmodern' society. Unfortunately, empirical research on urban change in the UK has yet to be properly informed by the postmodernism debate; partly, no doubt, because we are still some way from seeing agreement on what 'the condition of postmodernity' actually is!

8.7 An important contribution to our understanding of the links between the social and physical transformations of inner/central city neighbourhoods is provided by **Hamnett and Randolph** (1988). They describe and account for the process of tenurial change in central and inner London where privately rented blocks of flats have been broken up into separate properties and then sold for owner-occupation. The special features of this changeover from private rented accommodation to owner-occupation are that these are flats not houses, and that unlike private rented property elsewhere in England and Wales, these flats were often owned by large corporate landlords. However, the effect of the changeover is to bring about gentrification. 'The sale of privately rented property for high priced owner-occupation has led to the replacement of older, lower income households by younger, higher income buyers.'

8.8 The flat break-up for sale process began in the late 1960s. In 1966 only 6.4 of the private sector flats in central London were in owner-occupation, by 1981 this had-risen to 36.1%. Hamnett and Randolph explain this change as reflecting the high profitability of flat break-up, due to the capital gains achieved by transferring properties from a low capital value privately-rented sector (tenanted investment value), into the high capital value owner-occupation sector (vacant possession value). The reasons for the high value of properties in owner-occupation are many but include the ease of access to mortgage finance and the extraordinarily favourable tax regimes affecting both owner occupiers and building societies. This transfer of properties was facilitated by the emergence of the residential property trader who bought the block of flats 'wholesale' and sold individual flats 'retail', often assisting the purchasers to obtain mortgage finance. 'As a result of the activities of these . . . companies, the central London flat market was transformed in the space of five or six years (late 1960s and early 1970s) from genteel decline to one of the most dynamic and aggressive sectors of the property market.' The property boom came to an end in 1974, but the market picked up again after 1976 so that by the late 1970s there were no companies investing in the flat market for anything other than its break-up potential.

8.9 Hamnett and Randolph see certain social and physical changes resulting from this flat break-up process. The social changes are revealed in the occupational, wealth and age differences between owners and tenants after the transfer. The newcomer owners are younger, wealthier and in higher status occupations, than the sitting tenants who bought their flats (often on leasehold), who are in turn better off than the increasingly elderly remaining tenants. Physical modification often accompanies flat break-up because of the need to maximise the sale price of the property. But another physical change is, according to Hamnett and Randolph, consequent upon break-up. Whereas the previous owners were investment landlords who had an interest in maintaining the properties in good condition to protect their reputations as landlords, the new owners are primarily interested in income from the sales of flats. As a result standards of maintenance and repair have often deteriorated sharply and rents on the remaining tenancies have increased. Thus many tenants and leaseholders have good reason to view themselves as the victims of the flat break-up process.

8.9 This study of the flat break-up process nicely complements the flurry of research interest in the more 'classical' form of gentrification currently taking place in the London docklands.

8(ii) Political determinations of land use and built form; land use planning, new and expanded towns, green belts and development control; anti-growth coalitions

8.10 The landscapes of the cities are not only changed, however, by the unplanned social changes of the type discussed above, they are often modified through the application of the law, and the execution of explicit planning policies. An obvious instance of this is the attempt to achieve a 'containment of urban Britain' through the use of green belt legislation, but the effects of planning on the urban land use and built form can range enormously from the creating of manifestly planned landscapes, such as those found in the New Towns, to minor changes in the stock of urban facilities such as are achieved through the process of 'planning gain' (for example, when a developer builds and donates certain social facilities in return for planning permission to redevelop part of a city centre).

8.11 The manner and degree to which land use and environmental planning has shaped urban built form has attracted much research interest over the years. In particular, researchers have been concerned to define the 'limits of power' that planners experience in managing urban areas, and, through the analysis of detailed case studies, have shown the way that outcomes have often reflected compromises between planning principle and the interests of powerful groups and individuals.

8.12 Major themes in this research effort have been:

(i) the role of local plans in shaping land use development;

(ii) the success of new towns and the influence of new and expanded towns on industrial location;

(iii) the influence on outcomes of the manner in which key planning decisions are made, for example in the case of major developments such as the Sizewell B nuclear power station;

(iv) the effectiveness of green belt policies in containing urban growth;

(v) the manner in which conflicts of interests between developers, residents and local and central government are resolved in areas of high growth such as Berkshire; and

(vi) the role of environmental groups in shaping planning outcomes.

Other examples are, aesthetic control, bus deregulation and superstore location.

8.13 Perhaps the most authoritative work in this field in the recent period has been carried out by Patsy Healey and her colleagues. In their recent book (**Healey et al** 1988) they report on empirical research, conducted mostly in Greater Manchester and the West Midlands, into the nature and significance of planning as it is actually practised in contemporary Britain. They define the function of the Land Use Planning System as the mediation of conflicting production and consumption interests in respect of how land should be used and developed. Then, focusing on this mediation process, they discuss the effects of land use planning on the social and physical development of certain tracts within the two conurbations. They group their empirical studies under three headings: the city centre; the inner city; and the urban fringe. They find that the effect of planning in the city centre is that, through detailed negotiation between the planners and the commercial and public sector interests involved, a more efficient spatial organisation of the city centre is achieved, and its environmental quality and image are enhanced. Since they assume that this has the effect of sustaining land values, they claim that 'the planning system emerges as working through the negotiative practice of development control to insert into the considerations of individual landowners and developers a strategy which is in the collective interest of most parties who care about city centres.'(p72)

8.14   The situation in the inner city is, however, very different. Here, instead of mediating between local 'consumer' interests and those of private sector investors (as in the city centre or on the urban fringe), the planner is mediating between both producer and consumer interests and the many parts and programmes of public sector agencies. Planning is so limited in these areas by dwindling resources, an over dependence on the public sector, the almost insuperable problems of co-ordination between public sector agencies and a highly charged political environment, that, as Healey et al admit, 'many politicians, planners and other council officials doubt the value of statutory planning in the inner city.'(p97)

8.15   On the urban fringe, however, there is no problem of a shortage of private sector investment. Healey et al find that land use planning, responding to strongly represented 'consumer' interests, maintained containment, and channelled the development that was allowed into locations which impacted least upon the rural environment and upon those already resident in the areas. They claim that by this means 'the negotiation process . . . has sustained scarcity and quality.' They also found, however, that both developers and locals lost out when the 'consistency and continuity' of a development plan around which a consensus had formed was undermined by decisions taken outside the local area. This particularly relates to the Solihull area where piecemeal development of large sites at the urban fringe was permitted, often on appeal to the Secretary of State for the Environment, when such developments contravened local policies favouring planning restraint on green belt and environmental grounds.

8.16   This shift of influence from the local level to the centre is also evident in the chapter on 'open land' planning where the removal of the firm presumption in favour of agricultural land, and the use of the criterion of profitability (as for example in supporting the case of opencast coalmining) weakens the position of local interests when they line up against new developments in rural areas.

8.17   The picture which emerges from the detailed case studies is of planners struggling to achieve spatially efficient and socially desirable outcomes through patient negotiation with those actors and agencies — commercial and industrial firms, land developers and housebuilders, government departments and public sector agencies — whose activities impinge on the physical fabric of British cities. Their

efforts are often rewarded with some degree of success, and the book lacks that blanket pessimism found in Ambrose's 'Whatever Happened to Planning', but at the same time, there is a lot of evidence here to show that the changes of the last 10 years have made the planners task even more difficult than before.

8(iii) **The role of housing policy in shaping urban structures; urban renewal**

8.18   Cities are shaped not just by the policies and practise of town and country planning but by policies in many other areas, notably transport and housing. Housing policies are particularly important, they affect the location, volume and types of investment in both new housebuilding, and in housing improvement. The present Conservative government's housing policies have been widely criticised, and much of this criticism has been supported by academic research, which points to the socially regressive effects of council house sales, the 'privatisation of urban renewal', reduced levels of council house building, the 'chaos' of the housing benefit system, the tax subsidisation of home ownership and the deregulation of rented housing.

8.19   Some researchers, however, emphasise the continuity of policy pre- and post- 1979, and do not see a downturn in the prospects for those who live in poor housing in inner city areas. **Maclennan** (1985) adopts this more positive position in his evaluation of housing policies in Glasgow. He stresses in particular the key role of housing associations in the rehabilitation process, and the wider economic impacts of the programmes on the surrounding areas. His conclusions are 'that the housing association rehabilitation programme can have major redevelopment impacts on neighbourhoods, that the worst housing and poorest houses are the major beneficaries, that the rate of public subsidy to investment is extremely high, and that programme well-being has been, so far, only marginally influenced by government change. (And) . . . government, through sustaining a strong policy commitment has so far pursued a generally laudable strategy.' He shows that Glasgow, where the local authority favoured the use of housing associations, attracted 60% of Scottish Housing Corporation expenditure but had only 40% of the 'below tolerable standard' housing. This produced an intensity of rehabilitation spending unmatched in any other British city.

8.20   The reasons for seeing this Glasgow housing rehabilitation as an 'encouraging example' of British housing policy are many. Firstly, the process is locally managed with the tenants themselves playing an important role. Secondly, the benefits were reaching those who were most in need. The populations of the improved tenement housing were predominantly the elderly poor, and, of those in the economically active age groups, 37% were unemployed. Thirdly, the housing affected was inadequate; private investment in the properties had been virtually non-existent for decades, and the flats were poorly-equiped (65% lacked bath or shower) and in a very poor state of repair. Fourthly, the process of rehabilitation resulted in no displacement or gentrification. Indeed, far from owner-occupation replacing private renting, the level of owner-occupation actually went down from 43% to 10% as a result of the programmme. This was because poor owner-occupiers sold their properties to the housing association in preference to facing the (partial) costs of rehabilitation themselves. Finally, the benefits spread out beyond the areas undergoing rehabilitation. Maclennan shows that house prices in neighbouring areas increased rapidly and that significant numbers of jobs were created by the programme. He also suggests that this intensive public investment in the poorest areas may have constituted that critical level of investment needed to promote a longer-term self-sustaining regeneration based upon private sector confidence in the Glasgow economy.

8.21   A much less optimistic stance is taken by Tony Crook in his evaluation of the Conservative government's housing policies and in particular the effects of their policies for low-cost home ownership (**Crook** 1986). Crook points out that the sale of council houses to their tenants through their 'right-to-buy' represents far and away the largest element in the package of policies designed to extend home ownership to low income households. In the four years 1980–81 to 1983–84 over 500,000 council dwellings were sold in this way with another 5,000 dwellings coming from the housing associations. The other policies were very small in comparison: co-ownership/shared ownership schemes with housing associations brought 37,000 into owner occupation, local authorities built 25,000 houses for sale under license, and about 5,000 each were added by local authority shared ownership, homesteading, dwellings improved for sale by housing associations, and mortgages guaranteed by local authorities. Other schemes produced insignificant additions. Crook points out that council house sales provide resources for the promotion of other schemes to extend home ownership, but that the geographical distribution of the sales of council houses does not coincide with the areas with greatest housing need. The sales tend to be in the shire counties and in the South, whereas need is greatest in the metropolitan cities in the North.

8.22   Crook then assesses the impact of each of the policy measures. He joins others (notably Forrest and Murie, see section 3.4 above) in stating that the effects of the highly subsidised council house sales are:

(i)   to favour fairly well-off, middle-aged, skilled manual worker households with grown up children (i.e. not usually those in greatest need); and

(ii) to take out of the council stock much of the larger housing in the most accessible and/or attractive areas, (thus leaving only maisonettes and flats, most of them in inner city locations, for the next generation of council tenants).

With only a small number of properties involved, the impact of the other schemes is minimal. Shared ownership schemes have tended to favour smaller households and especially divorced, separated and widowed women. Such schemes are highly concentrated in South East England. Improvement for sale and homesteading are more likely to occur in areas where housing needs are greatest, that is in the inner areas of large northern cities, but again the numbers benefiting are very small. The cheapest new houses being built are those in starter home and build for sale schemes. Some of these developments took place on cleared sites in inner city locations and high hopes were entertained that this would become the norm. But in fact most starter homes are built on greenfield sites outside the inner city. The beneficiaries of new starter homes tend to be young people both single and couples, and more than a third were under the age of 25. Other build for sale houses have more varied buyers and when located in the inner city they attract outsiders as well as local residents. Crook summarises as follows:

> 'These new initiatives help people to buy cheaper houses. They help existing older households to buy good quality housing from the older stock without substantial increases in their household budget. They help newly formed households to get new houses earlier than they would have done and thus stimulate a market for new houses.'

He adds, however, that it is hard to see these programmes as creating net new investment, and that the beneficiaries are rarely those in most need. Furthermore, it is one thing to get lower income people into owner-occupation, quite another to ensure that these people will be able to afford the upkeep of their homes. And it is because of the need for much more investment by low income home-owners in the maintenance and repair of their properties that Crook concludes by saying that paradoxically the privatisation of housing creates the need for more public expenditure rather than less. If this support is not forthcoming there will be a serious decline in the quality of the national housing stock.

Evaluation

8.22   Our evaluation of the research on the effects of social change, politics and policies on the built environment and the urban system are as follows:

(i) on gentrification, we accept the significance of the growth of the service class in producing change in the inner city. However, more needs to be known about individual housing and labour market careers before gentrification can be viewed as a permanent feature of UK urban change. Specifically, do the newcomers stay, or do they leave for the suburbs to be replaced by younger versions of themselves? We also need to know more about the social impact of gentrification, especially on working class households. We would argue that it is not sufficient to assume that labour markets impact on a passive housing market. This would imply that gentrification is explained by the growth of producer services employment in the centres of the major cities. Rather it is quite possible that gentrification is itself affecting the nature of local labour markets and what kinds of new investment occur there. Finally, we need to know more about the implications of gentrification for political change. Does it shift the areas affected from the left towards the centre or right, or from the 'old left' towards the 'new'? And

(ii) on the role of state intervention in shaping built form, we would suggest that there has not yet been a fully considered assessment of the ways in which the reduction in public expenditure and in planning authority has affected development outcomes. As this phase of urban planning policy reaches the end of its first decade, the questions which arise are: what has been the effect on the volume of construction? Has the regional/sub-regional balance of construction changed? What has been the effect on regional/sub-regional house prices and business rents? Which groups have been disadvantaged by the shift in development planning from social ethic to business ethic? Is the state getting a better financial deal from the new policies or are covert subsidies to the private sector allowing more public money to be diverted?

CHAPTER 9

The role of social relations, policy and culture in shaping urban economic performance

9.1 Our last chapter raises some of the most central questions about urban change in the UK in the recent period. It reviews research which explores the ways in which the economic performance of cities and regions has been affected by social and cultural factors, and by the state, both central and local, through urban and regional development policies.

relations left behind by previous rounds of investment. Does the research literature successfully operationalise this idea? Can one identify the sedimented social and cultural effects of past rounds of investment? With what confidence can one explain the trajectories of urban economic development today in terms of these social histories?

Issues

9.2 (i) How far have local and central state policies affected the nature and performance of local economies? What has been the impact of explicit urban and regional development policies such as the designation of Development Areas, and the setting up of Enterprise Zones and Urban Development Corporations? Do other state policies, for example defence policy, have spatial implications? Does the level of business rates have an affect on industrial location and profitability? Do transport policies affect employment levels and economic performance?

(ii) What are the implications for economic development, of the local and regional cultures discussed in Chapter 7? Do certain areas exhibit an 'enterprise culture', while others are burdened with a 'culture of dependency'? If so, what effects do these different values systems have on the level and type of urban economic activity? and

(iii) One of the most powerful integrating concepts developed in the recent period to explain urban and regional change in Britain has been that of 'spatial divisions of labour'. Central to this conceptual scheme is the idea that successive rounds of investment relate to the social structures and cultural and political

Contributions

9.3 The contributions to this field of research are grouped under five headings:

(i) general studies of the impact of the political process on urban and regional development; public sector spending; small firms support;

(ii) evaluations of the effects of regional policy;

(iii) the impact of urban policy on economic performance; Urban Development Corporations, Enterprise Zones . . ;

(iv) 'local socialism' — evaluations of its effects, local government economic policies; and

(v) social bases of economic development; socialisation and education; 'enterprise cultures'; local proactivity; the 'combination of layers'.

9(i) General studies of the impact of the political process on urban and regional development; public sector spending; small firms support

9.4 Evaluations of government policies affecting Britain's urban and regional economies abound. They fall into a number of categories. Firstly, there are those that are concerned primarily with industrial policy. Most of these are highly critical of the present Conservative government which they argue has helped to create an industrial wasteland in much of northern and western Britain (and to redefine the 'north' so that it now includes the West Midlands region). But some of the more thoughtful contributors recognise that government industrial policies before 1979 were also responsible for causing unemployment and economic disruption. For example, the reorganization policies in nationalised industries such as steel and coal had helped to 'wreck' several regions during the post-war period. The Government is also criticised for not putting sufficient resources into industrial innovation (especially in information and communications technology), or into youth training.

9.5   Secondly, considerable research effort has been directed at evaluating the urban and regional effects of the Conservative government's attempts to reduce public expenditure. Some studies are pitched at a fairly general level and examine, for example, the role of the public sector in urban employment change, or levels of urban service provision. Others focus on specific issues such as health service restructuring, school closures or social welfare (single payments). An active research area in the recent period has been that of the urban and regional allocation of public expenditures, and of the pattern of central grants to local government. Sometimes this is linked to analyses of levels of tax income obtained from different areas and more specifically the urban effects of change in the system of local taxation, for example, the establishment of a uniform business rate. Finally, considerable research effort has been directed towards those areas of policy which have particular significance for urban change, notably transport policy (motorway investments, the issue of road user charges), office development policy and tourism policy.

9.6   Fairly typical of competent and thoughtful empirical research on government policy as it effects urban and regional economic development, is that carried out by Mason and Harrison on the regional impact of the Government's financial assistance to small firms (**Mason and Harrison** 1986). The authors investigate the regional take-up rates of four forms of assistance — the Small Firm Loan Guarantee Scheme (under which bank loans to small firms are guaranteed by the government); the Business Expansion Scheme (which offers tax advantages to investors in new equity of unquoted UK companies); the Small Engineering Investment Scheme (which provides grants for the use of advanced machinery in engineering workshops); and the Enterprise Allowance Scheme (which tops up benefit to those unemployed who try to set themselves up in business or become self-employed). It was intended that the financial assistance to small firms

would display high 'additionality', that is, that the benefits would go to promote investments which would not otherwise have been made. Since those firms and individuals which operate in the South East region and in southern England more generally are well-placed by this fact to obtain finance (for example, through using housing as collateral, or because of the prosperous local markets for their products or services), it might be expected that the northern and western regions would be more than averagely represented in the take-up of these forms of government assistance. Mason and Harrison show that this is not the case. The general picture was one in which the South East and East Anglia, and the South West and East Midlands regions were particularly high on take-up, and the northern and western regions were low. Variations occurred between one scheme and another, for example, the Loan Guarantee Scheme had a large number of users in the North West region, perhaps because the National Westminster Bank had been particularly active in promoting it there. But, in general, the spatial pattern of use of these forms of assistance fairly closely matched that of the index of regional entrepreneurship developed by Storey in 1982, which peaked in the south and east and dipped in the north and west (see 9.23 below). Mason and Harrison point out that by this means the policy for supporting small firms, though national in scope, actually serves to boost economic activity in those areas which are already privileged, and that it therefore runs counter to the purposes of regional policy. They also point out, however, that to evaluate the policies fully, one would need to know, not only if levels of additionality varied between places, but also if there were differences in the degree to which the assisted firms displaced production and jobs from other firms in their areas. One would also need to know what the regional failure rates of the small firms were (nationally, the failure rate for the Loan Guarantee Scheme is very high at nearly 40% after three years).

9(ii)   **Evaluations of the effects of regional policy**

9.7   In the previous section we discussed a study which showed that a non-spatial policy (financial assistance to small firms) nevertheless had unintended spatial outcomes (and ones which contradicted regional policy). In this section we review literature on the role of regional policy itself in effecting a redistribution of employment opportunities in favour of the industrial conurbations and regions of northern and western Britain (and Northern Ireland). Much of the research takes its lead from work carried out in the early-mid 1970s by Barry Moore and John Rhodes, which came to the conclusion (in ways discussed below) that government regional policy during the 1960s had been highly successful in generating jobs in the development (assisted) areas by diverting manufacturing investment there through a combination of measures, notably controls on land development for industry in the South East, investment incentives and an employment subsidy. Three kinds of critical response to this argument can be identified. The first questioned the results on the basis that the estimation procedures were inadequate. The second rejected the interpretation placed on the results by claiming that it was for reasons other than state regional policy (notably labour shortages) that firms were investing in northern and western regions. The third argued that, even at the height of regional policy, governments were on balance favouring the southern regions of Britain because of the spatial bias in that direction to be found in their other programmes (notably defence procurement).

9.8   In 1986 **Moore, Rhodes and Tyler** published a report for the DTI which updated their earlier work to cover the period 1961–1981. They began by reviewing studies in the evaluation of regional policy and by summarising the developments in regional policy over the 20 years, emphasising the fact that the policy instruments changed significantly over this period, notably because Industrial Development Certificates (IDCs) and the Regional Employment Premium (REP) were wound up and Regional Selective Assistance (RSA) introduced. Their methods of estimating the effects of regional policy are as follows: they calculate the employment levels in the four main development areas which would be expected on the basis of each industry in those areas growing at that industry's national rate, (equivalent to the structural component in the shift-share analysis). This expected employment is then compared with the actual and the difference curve is plotted. This curve shows a sudden rise in the early-mid 1960s, peaking in the mid 1970s, then declining in the early 1980s. By extrapolating the curve of the 'passive policy period' (1950–63) into the later periods, the authors are able to calculate the extra jobs arising in the 'active policy period' (divided into those created in the indigenous sector of the regional economies and those arising from 'immigrant' investments). The figure they arrive at is 450,000 jobs due to regional policy over the period 1961–81, of which nearly two-thirds were created in the first decade.

9.9   Disentangling the effects of specific regional policy instruments they estimate that about 310,000 of the net gain of 450,000 jobs were due to investment incentives, that IDCs accounted for another 70,000, and that the remainder were due to RSA and REP. Possessing the estimates of jobs created by policy instrument and the cost to the Government of the policies, allows the authors to calculate costs per job (lowest for IDC (virtually costless), low for RSA and highest for REP). They then calculate the impact of regional policy at the sub-regional level and by industry, showing that four industries, mechanical engineering, electrical engineering, vehicles and clothing were in

receipt of 27% of the grants paid but generated 50% of the total regional policy jobs. Finally, they estimate labour market balance sheets for the Development Area regions, all other regions and for the UK as a whole, for the 1951–81 period.

9.10   The significance of this report is not just that they feel they make a convincing case for an active regional policy in the 1980s and 90s, but their claim, based upon their statistical analyses, that jobs created by regional policy in the 1961–81 period accounted for 28% of employment in the Development Areas in 1981.

9(iii) The impact of urban policy on economic performance; Urban Development Corporations, Enterprise Zones...

9.11   The Moore, Rhodes and Tyler report claimed that the Government's regional policy measures helped to produce the rapid decline of manufacturing employment in London, assisted the maintenance of manufacturing employment levels in the largest conurbations of the Development Area regions, but had its most positive impact on the non metropolitan areas in northern and western Britain. In this way regional policy is seen to be having urban impacts. However, during the post-war period there has been an increasing commitment by governments to a specifically urban economic rejuvenation policy. The history of this sphere of policy-making has been written by Paul Lawless ('Urban Growth and Change in Britain'); and Brian Robson ('Those Inner Cities') and David Donnison ('Regenerating the Inner City') have contributed useful evaluations of recent policy initiatives. But careful analyses of specific urban economic policy instruments are also appearing now.

9.12   A good example of such research is that carried out by **PA Cambridge Economic Consultants** for the DoE on the Enterprise Zone (EZ) experiment. The EZs were set up in 1981 to bring about the physical redevelopment of areas characterised by industrial decline. To attract new investment in these areas firms were offered a package of benefits, of which the three most important were rate exemption for ten years following designation of the EZ, capital allowances whereby firms could set all of their capital expenditure in the EZ against tax, and a streamlined planning system with minimum bureaucratic constraints placed upon those investing in the EZ. The EZs were set up in two rounds, 10 of them in 1981–2, and a further 13 in 1983–4. PACEC find that the net exchequer costs of the programme were a considerable £300 million over the first four years, half of which was due to capital allowances and the rest due to rate relief, and infrastructure and land acquisition costs. Since the programme led to the creating of an estimated net increase of 13,000 jobs in the EZ local economies, the cost per job works out at about £23,000. The figure of 13,000 new jobs is much lower than the total of 63,000 people employed in EZs in 1986. This is because nearly half of these were in establishments which were there when the EZ was designated, and over half of the remainder were due to local transfers of businesses into the EZ. Unusually, there is some attempt to discuss the 'replacement' effects of the investments. 63% of all employment in EZs in 1986 were in manufacturing, but retailing, distribution and the construction industry were also important. Indeed the research includes a case study of the impact in the Swansea area of the location of a major shopping centre in the Swansea EZ.

9.13 The benefits of the EZ policy are not always retained by the businesses located there. The rate relief advantages are recouped by the landlords through higher rents, and the capital allowances by firms whose head offices were often outside the area. However, the physical improvement of the areas seems to have had an important economic and psychological impact, and has benefited those firms located in the surrounding areas as well. The EZs in the south and midlands have achieved the fastest rate of development, and PACEC consider that there has been some 'dead weight' here, in the sense that the financial assistance has gone to firms who were likely to make their investments in that area in any case, (this is especially true for retailing investments). PACEC's conclusions therefore are 'that real benefits are being provided to designated zones and their surrounding local economies, (but that) the cost effectiveness of the experiment could be improved by reducing the amount of 'dead weight' on both capital allowances and rate relief, which could be differentiated across zones and between economic sectors or 'tapered' downwards through time.'

9.14 Similiar kinds of evaluative research have been conducted on other government urban economic policies, such as the Urban Development Corporations, Task Forces, Urban Programme, etc. The special programmes operated by the Scottish and Welsh Development Offices have also received attention. Local authorities' industrial development initiatives have been actively researched despite the limited resources that they command and one of the issues raised has been the significance of the political complexion of the local authority in determining the type and strengths of policies implemented. A related issue is that of the lack of local accountability posed by certain instruments of urban policy, such as the Urban Development Corporations. Also, since such development often provides jobs for people living in the suburbs and housing for newcomer middle-class households, the question which is often raised is who benefits from urban policy? The fear that urban policy is not sufficiently targeted to those most in need is nicely expressed in the call for 'local jobs and local houses for local people.'

9.15 The three policy evaluation studies reviewed so far, although they contain certain criticisms of government thinking and action, nevertheless assume that governments are genuinely keen to solve urban and regional development problems, to reduce social and spatial inequalities, and in particular to improve the living standards and life chances of the poorest sections of the population. It would be quite wrong, however, to leave the impression that this is true for all academic writing on urban change in Britain. Two versions of a much more fundamentally critical perspective exist. In the first and milder version, emphasis is placed on the political necessity for governments to be seen to doing something about urban poverty. The resulting policies are interpreted as performing the role of palliatives — they alleviate the 'pain' without addressing the cause of the 'illness'. The harsher version borders on a conspiracy theory; it asserts that governments have a 'hidden agenda' in carrying out urban policy and that they know that their actions cannot and will not significantly improve conditions for the urban poor.

9.16 A good example of this latter kind of writing is provided by Sills, Taylor and Golding, in their book on the Inner Area Programme in Leicester (**Sills, Taylor and Golding** 1988). They arrive at some very pessimistic conclusions concerning the nature and effects of the Inner Areas Programme (IAP). The IAP is seen as a poverty programme and, as such, it is judged to have both an official justification and a 'hidden agenda'. Its objective is said to be to tackle urban poverty, but Sills et al consider that it is really designed to maintain public order and consent (they refer in part to the riots in 1981 and 1985). As an area-based policy it is supposed to tackle poverty in those areas in which that process is especially concentrated. But the problem is that the degree of that concentration is quite limited and most poor people live outside programme authorities. So perhaps the more compelling reason for an area-based policy is because the threat to public order is urban, indeed, inner urban, based. Similarly the poverty programmes are small scale, as if the poverty itself was small scale, when in fact it is widespread and requires expensive national action. Sills et al also doubt the innovatory or experimental nature of the programmes, and the fact that they take the form of a programme of projects. This appears to allow direct contact with those in need, but can actually act as a vehicle for political patronage. Finally, their view of joint funding is that this is not to do with partnership, but is to ensure central control on the broad features of the allocation of funds.

9.17 Sills et al. then try to provide evidence to support this critical stance in relation to the Leicester IAP. They point out how insignificant the resources were in relation to the size of the problem, and indeed how the extra monies made available through the programme failed to match the resources lost through public expenditure cuts. They describe the financial and management problems which accompanied projects initiated by the voluntary sector, and the problems of securing agreement on common objectives between different agencies. Through an interview survey of those who applied for IAP funding in Leicester, the authors found out how frustrated many became by the process of applying for funds, and when they heard, as 75% of applicants did, that they had been unsuccessful in their bids. The competition for support seemed to set one group off against another, white against black, old against young. And hostility towards the Council was common. Sills et al conclude by saying that 'all such (inner city) programmes have been rich in rhetoric.' Ten years after the inception of the IAP it is clear that it has not succeeded in 'reversing the engine of decline and exodus' in the inner city. The attraction of poverty programmes, according to Sills et al, 'is their ability to offer a high-profile, low cost legitimation exercise for governments unwilling to face up to the resource implications involved in really tackling urban deprivation.'

9(iv) 'Local socialism' - evaluations of its effects; local government economic policies

9.18 An increasing number of left-wing Labour administrations appeared in Britain's major cities during the early 1980s. These councils attempted to achieve a form of 'local socialism' in their areas — to put into practise locally the alternative economic strategies which would form the basis of central government policies when Labour was returned to power in Westminster. Though rather dated now (1984), the collection of essays edited by **Boddy and Fudge** and called 'Local Socialism' is a useful source of information and ideas about the role of local government in local economic development. Two of the chapters in the book refer to the dual state hypothesis (discussed in section 7(vii) above), where the emphasis is on local authorities as the providers of consumption goods and services. But in Martin Boddy's chapter on Local Economic and Employment Strategies, the emphasis is elsewhere — on the role of Labour local authorities in promoting changes which would reduce unemployment, and generally improve economic and employment prospects within their areas.

9.19 Boddy begins by describing the usual ways in which local authorities assisted economic development, notably through the provision of sites and premises, through promotion, advertising and advice, and financially (though on a very small scale) through grants and loans. The character of such assistance to private enterprise was that it was property-led, business-oriented, relatively unconcerned with employment promotion or the interests of disadvan-

taged groups, competitive with other local authorities, and geared towards the small firm sector.

9.20 He then contrasts this with the radical interventions of a small number of Labour local authorities (notably Sheffield City Council, West Midlands County Council and the Greater London Council) in the early 1980s. The younger and more radical councillors in charge of these councils drew upon the experience of the Labour administration's National Enterprise Board, the CDP lessons, the much admired Lucas Aerospace shop stewards movement, and the thinking which was being fed into the Left's alternative economic strategy. Boddy analyses the policies and practices of the three radical authorities, from which he draws some general conclusions. While largely defensive in character in the face of recession, the interventions were novel in that they prioritised the interests of workers rather than owners. The councils were engaging in 'propaganda by example', illustrating alternatives to Conservative policies to develop support for socialist principles: 'In this sense bottom-up, popular planning, involving union and locality-based groups, new forms of work organisation and control, and the exploratory work in relation to new technology and socially useful production, are central'. They were also testing out some of the ideas that might form part of a national Alternative Economic Strategy (for example, trying to draw upon the vast resources of the pension funds for socially responsible investment). Boddy also claims that the initiatives usefully contested the usual distinction between economic (national) policy and social (local) policy.

9.21 Boddy then turns to the problems and pitfalls of these radical interventions. The main one, of course, was the insignificance of the benefits of these policies in relation to the size of the problem — the local authorities could claim gains of only a few hundred jobs, in the face of unemployment running into the millions. But, in addition, there is the dilemma that the local economic policies will finish up supporting local capital rather than serving to advance socialist forms of production and organisation (such as co-operatives, 'popular planning' etc.). Finally, if the radical councils are to persuade others to become socially responsive and responsible in their attitudes and practices, they must first put their own houses in order (for example in their recruitment behaviours).

9(v) Social bases of economic development: socialisation and education - 'enterprise cultures'; local pro-activity; the 'combination of layers'

9.22 This Chapter has until now discussed the way that the social and the political impact on the economic solely in terms of the role of state intervention and state policy. But, although this receives a great deal of attention by researchers, it is not the whole or even, perhaps, the larger part of the way that urban economic performance is affected by social, political and cultural forces.

9.23   The idea that the social structures and cultural values of an area have an influence on its current economic development has a long history, even if sometimes it seems that it is a recent discovery. Checkland, for example, in his studies of Scottish economic history refers to the 'Upas Tree' effect (this Indonesian tree is thought to have the ability to poison the growth of any competing tree in its vicinity). By analogy, the nineteenth century rapid urbanisation of Glasgow, based upon shipbuilding, engineering and textiles, resulted in large establishments, employing a militant proletarianised workforce. This discouraged both new inward investment, and the emergence of new business initiatives from within the area. Hence the loss of economic dynamism over a large part of west-central Scotland.

9.24   The rediscovery of the idea that urban economic change is partly, but fundamentally, a function of the values and attitudes of an area's population, and that different social class structures tend to imply different economic possibilities, is due largely to the work of **Doreen Massey** (1985). Massey's book 'Spatial Divisions of Labour' is mostly about changes in the organisation of production which result in a changing industrial geography of Britain. But on several occasions she discusses the way that the restructuring process is itself subject to the social relations left behind by previous rounds of accumulation. In relation to unskilled and semi-skilled electronics workers, she argues that on the whole wages are lower, the degree of trade union organisation weaker, and things such as absenteeism lower, where such workers have had less of a history of employment in capitalist wage relations. There are locational advantages, therefore, for investment 'where there are reserves of new workers coming on to the capitalist labour market for the first time'. A number of areas have such reserves, in particular of female labour (for example, the old coal/steel industrial areas, small towns in rural areas, and tourist resorts). In contrast, the high status workers (for example, those working on research and development) are in a privileged position. They readily move between companies but within high amenity regions such as the British sunbelt to the west of and around London. 'Work follows them not vice versa'. 'Both for social reasons and as a result of the nature of the labour market, these groups ... tend to cluster together in small and highly defined parts of the country, usually well away from manual workers and production as such, and have power thereby to influence industrial location (and) the economic geography of the country'.

9.25   On the basis of such considerations, Massey asserts that 'the form and direction of the change that results from the insertion of a local area into a new division of labour, will depend on the existing character of the area, itself the result of an already long and complex history'. 'What takes place is the interrelation of the new spatial structure with the accumulated results of the old. The 'combination' of layers, in other words, really does mean combination, with each side of the process affecting the other'.

Evaluation

9.26   Our evaluation of the literature reviewed in this Chapter is as follows:

(i) we feel that using only industrial structure and policy to analyse the impact of regional policy is inadequate since the differential performance of cities and regions could in fact be caused by any number of factors (for example the spatial reorganisation of production, or relative wage levels);

(ii) we became convinced of the importance of variation in local private and public sector institutions, and in local political cultures in mediating the effects of national policies in local areas. What is more, an enterprise culture can take many forms; and

(iii) on the role of social structures in economic performance, we endorse the emphasis on spatial divisions of labour, and on the importance of the 'combination of layers' of past rounds of accumulation in affecting present patterns of urban and regional development.

Bibliography

ADAMS, C.D., BAUM, A.E. and MACGREGOR, B.D. (1985), The influence of valuation practices upon the price of vacant inner city land. *Land Development Studies*, 2(3), 157–173. 1(iv)

ASHTON, D.N., MAGUIRE, M.J. and SPILSBURY, M. (1988), Local labour markets and their impacts on the life chances of youths. In Coles, R. (ed), *Young Careers*. Milton Keynes: Open University Press. 4(x).

BARLOW, J. and SAVAGE, M. (1986), The other side of Mrs Thatcher's high-tech Utopia. University of Sussex, Urban and Regional Studies Working Papers. 5(iii).

BENYON, J. and SOLOMOS, J. (eds) (1987), *The Roots of Urban Unrest*, Oxford: Pergamon. 7(v).

BOAL, F.W. (1982), Segregating and mixing: space and residence in Belfast, In Boal, F.W. et al. (eds), *Integration and Division: Geographical Perspectives on the Northern Ireland Problem*. London: Academic Press. 7(ii).

BODDY, M. and FUDGE, C. (eds) (1984), *Local Socialism*. Basingstoke: Macmillan. 9(iv).

CHAMPION, A.G. and GREEN, A.E. (1988), Rating places: winners and losers in 1980s Britain. Mimeo. 1(i).

CHESHIRE, P.C. and HAY, D.G. (1988), *Urban Problems in Europe*. London: Allen and Unwin. 1(iii).

COLEMAN, A. (1985), *Utopia on Trial: Vision and Reality in Planned Housing*. London: Shipman. 3(i).

COOKE, P.N. (ed) (1986), *Global Restructuring: Local Response*. London: ESRC. 6(i).

COOKE, P.N. (ed) (1989), *Localities*. London: Unwin Hyman. 6(i).

CROOK, A.D.H. (1986), The privatisation of housing and the impact of the Conservative government's housing policies. *Environment and Planning*, A18, 639–659, etc. 8(iii).

CROSS, M. and JOHNSON, M. (1988), Mobility denied: Afro-Caribbean labour and the British economy. In Cross, M. and Entzinger, H. (eds), 1988, *Lost Illusions: Caribbean Minorities in Britain and the Netherlands*. London: Routledge. 4(xii).

CURTIS, S. and MOHAN, J. (1989), The geography of ill-health and health care. In Lewis, J. and Townsend, A. (eds), 1989, *The North-South Divide: Regional Change in Britain in the 1980s*. London: Paul Chapman. 7(iii).

DALE, A. (1987), The effect of life cycle on three dimensions of stratification. In Bryman, A. et al. (eds), *Rethinking the Life Cycle*. London: Macmillan. 7(i).

DANIELS, P.W. (1985), *Service Industries*. Cambridge: UP. 4(vii).

DICKENS, P.G. et al. (1985), *Housing, States and Localities*. London: Methuen. 5(ii).

FOORD, J. and LEWIS, J. (1984), New gender relations and new towns in old industrial areas: women's employment in Peterlee and East Kilbride. *Built Environment* 10(1). 2(ii).

FORREST, R. and MURIE, A. (1986), *Selling the Welfare State: the Privatisation of Council Housing.* London: Croom Helm. 3(iv).

FOTHERGILL, S. and GUDGIN, G. (1983), Trends in regional manufacturing employment: the main influences. In Goddard, J.B. and Champion, A.G. (eds), 1983, *The Urban and Regional Transformation of Britain.* London: Methuen. 2(iv).

FRYER, D. and ULLAH, P., (eds) (1987), *Unemployed People: Social and Psychological Perspectives.* Milton Keynes: Open University Press. 6(iii).

GALLIE, D. (1985), The SCEL initiative: a provisional overview. In OPCS, OP34, British Society for Population Studies, Conference Paper. 6(i).

GODDARD, J.B. and GILLESPIE, A.E. (1986), Advanced telecommunications and regional economic development. In Robson, B.T. (ed), 1986, *Managing the City: the Aims and Impacts of Urban Policy.* London: Croom Helm. 5(i).

GOLDTHORPE, J., LLEWELLYN, C., and PAYNE, C. (1987) (2nd Edition), *Social Mobility and Class Structure in Modern Britain,* Oxford: Clarendon Press. 7(i).

GORDON, I.R. (1987), The structural element in regional unemployment. In Gordon, I.R. (ed), 1987, *Unemployment, the Regions and Labour Markets: Reactions to Recession.* London: Pion. 4(iv).

GREEN, A.E. (1986), The likelihood of becoming and remaining unemployed in GB 1984, *Transactions IBG,* NS11, 37–56. 4(iv).

HALCROW FOX and Associates/Birkbeck College, University of London (1986), Investigating Population Change in Small to Medium Sized Urban Areas. London: DoE.1(ii).

HAMNETT, C. and RANDOLPH, W. (1988), *Cities, Housing and Profits: the Flat Break-up Market in London* 8(i).

HAUSNER, V.A. (ed) (1986), *Urban Economic Change: Five City Studies.* Oxford: OUP. 4(ii).

HAUSNER, V.A. (ed) (1986), *Critical Issues in Urban Economic Development,* Vol.I. Oxford: Clarendon Press. 4(ii).

HEALEY, P. et al (eds) (1988), *Land Use Planning and the Mediation of Urban Change.* Cambridge: CUP. 8(ii).

HILLIER, B. and HANSON, J. (1984), *The Social Logic of Space.* Cambridge: CUP. 3(i).

JACKSON, P. (1989), *Maps of Meaning.* London: Unwin Hyman. 7(iv).

JOHNSTON, R. and PATTIE, C. (1989), Voting in Britain since 1979: a growing north-south divide? In Lewis, J., and Townsend, A. (eds), 1989, *The North-South Divide: Regional Change in Britain in the 1980s.* London: Paul Chapman. 7(vi).

KARN, V., KEMENY, J. and WILLIAMS, P. (1985), *Home Ownership in the Inner City: Salvation or Despair?* Aldershot: Gower. 3(ii).

KEEBLE, D. (1980), Industrial decline, regional policy and the urban-rural manufacturing shift in the UK. *Environment and Planning,* A 12, 945–62. 4(v).

LASH, S. and URRY, J. (1987), *The End of Organised Capitalism.* Cambridge: Polity Press. 6(i).

LEYSHON, A., DANIELS, P.W. and THRIFT, N.J. (1987), Working papers on producer services, 2, 4, and 5. University of Bristol/Liverpool. 4(viii).

LLOYD, P.E. and DICKEN, P. (1983), The components of change in metropolitan areas: events in their corporate context. In Goddard, J.D. and Champion A.G. (eds), 1983, *The Urban and Regional Transformation of Britain.* London: Methuen. 4(v).

MACLENNAN, D. (1985), Urban housing rehabilitation: an encouraging example. *Policy and Politics,* 13. 8(ii).

MARSHALL, G. et al. (1988), *Social Class in Modern Britain.* London: Hutchinson. 7(i).

MASON, C.M. and HARRISON, R.T. (1986), The regional impact of public policy towards small firms in the UK. In Keeble, D. and Wever, E. (eds), 1986, *New Firms and Regional Development in Europe.* London: Croom Helm. 9(i).

MASSEY, D. (1985), *Spatial Divisions of Labour: Social Structures and the Geography of Production.* London: Macmillan. 9(v).

MASSEY, D. and MEEGAN, R.A. (1982), *The Anatomy of Job Loss: the How, Why and Where of Employment Decline.* London: Methuen. 4(v).

MEEGAN, R. (1989), Paradise postponed: the growth and decline of Merseyside's outer estates. In Cooke, P., *Localities.* London: Unwin Hyman. 6(ii).

MINFORD, P., PEEL, M. and ASHTON, P. (1987), *The Housing Morass: Regulation, Immobility and Unemployment*. London: Institute of Economic Affairs. 2(i).

MOORE, B., RHODES, J. and TYLER, P. (1986), *The effects of Government Regional Policy*. London: HMSO. 9(ii).

MORGAN, K. and SAYER, R.A. (1988), *Microcircuits of Capital: the Electronics Industry and Uneven Development*. Cambridge: Polity Press. 4(vi).

MORRIS, L.D. (1987), Domestic circumstances. In Harris, C.C. et al. *Redundancy and Recession in South Wales*. Oxford: Blackwell. 6(iii).

PA CAMBRIDGE ECONOMIC CONSULTANTS (1987), *An Evaluation of the Enterprise Zone Experiment*. ICRP, HMSO. 9(iii).

PAHL, R.E. (1984), *Divisions of Labour*. Oxford: Blackwell. 6(ii).

PAHL, R.E. (1989), *On Work*. Oxford: Blackwell. 4(i).

PARKINSON, M. (1985), *Liverpool on the Brink*. London: Policy Journals. 7(vii).

POLLERT, A. (1988), Dismantling flexibility. *Capital and Class*, 34, 42–75. 4(ix).

ROBINS, K, and HEPWORTH, M. (1988), Home interactive telematics and the urbanisation process. In Williams, R. et al. (eds), 1988, *The Social Implications of Home Interactive Telematics*. Amsterdam: North-Holland.5(i)

SAUNDERS, P.R. (1984), Beyond housing classes. *International Journal of Urban and Regional Research*, 8(2). 3(iii).

SILLS, A., TAYLOR, G., and GOLDING, P. (1988), *The Politics of the Urban Crisis*. London: Hutchinson. 9(iii).

SMITH, S.J. (1986), *Crime, Space and Society*. Cambridge: CUP. 7(v).

STILLWELL, J.C.H., BODEN, P. and REES, P. (1988), Internal migration change in the UK: trends based on NHSCR movement data, 1975–6 to 1985–6. Regional Science Association conference paper. 1(ii).

VICKERMAN, R.W. (1987), The Channel Tunnel: consequences for regional growth and development. *Regional Studies*, 21(3), 187–98. 2(iii).

WALLMAN, S. (1984), *Eight London Households*. London: Tavistock. 7(iv).

WHITEHAND, J.W.R. (1987), *The Changing Face of Cities: A study of Development Cycles and Urban Form*. Oxford: Blackwell. 1(iv).

INDEX

Printed in the United Kingdom for HMSO.
Dd.292596, 6/90, C10, 3385/4, 5673, 103123.